new *food*

from the new basics to the new classics

new

food

from the new basics to the new classics

JILL DUPLEIX

photography by john hay and mark chew

MITCHELL
BEAZLEY

First published in 1994 by Mitchell Beazley International
part of Reed Consumer Books Ltd
Michelin House, 81 Fulham Road
London SW3 6RB

Originally published in 1994 by William Heinemann Australia
a part of Reed Books Australia
22 Salmon Street, Port Melbourne, Victoria 3207
a division of Reed International Books Australia Pty Limited

A CIP catalogue record for this book is available from the British Library
ISBN 1 85732 444 7

Typeset in 12 pt New Baskerville by Bookset
Printed and bound by Mandarin Offset

Conversion measurements for cups and spoons

Australian	British and North American
Liquids	
1 cup	250 ml/8 fl oz
1 tablespoon	15 ml
1 teaspoon	5 ml
Solids	
1 cup	$1\frac{1}{4}$ cups
$\frac{3}{4}$ cup	1 cup
$\frac{2}{3}$ cup	$\frac{3}{4}$ cup
$\frac{1}{2}$ cup	$\frac{2}{3}$ cup
$\frac{1}{3}$ cup	$\frac{1}{2}$ cup
$\frac{1}{4}$ cup	$\frac{1}{3}$ cup
2 tablespoons	$\frac{1}{4}$ cup
1 tablespoon	3 teaspoons

C O N T E N T S

with discussions on

the
credo

Buy only what is fresh and in season.

Do everything in your power to retain the original flavour of the produce.

Have fun.

Reach for the olive oil instead of the butter, and for the butter instead of the butter substitutes.

Question all cook books, including this one.

Don't shop ahead of time. Shop for now.

Share the preparing and cooking of food with family and friends.

Drink lots of water.

Buy the best quality food you can afford, and do less to it.

Eat cake. Sweet treats are not wicked, nor are they sinful. They are there to be enjoyed in small doses, in the context of a meal or a well balanced diet.

Make every meal an event, in some small but meaningful way.

Trust your instincts, not your recipes.

If you do eat meat, respect the animal it came from. As the Chinese say, don't kill it twice by not cooking it with respect. And try not to be a culinary hypocrite, aghast at the thought of fish heads, whole birds and offal, but happy to eat fish fillets, chicken sausages, and 'the best cut'.

Always go to the heart of the flavour.

Use sugar and honey where appropriate. At least they are natural products, not figments of a chemical engineer's imagination.

Don't diet. Instead, eat better food with more flavour, get heaps of exercise, and take a good, long look at your attitude to body image and self-esteem.

Remind yourself constantly that mistakes can be delicious.

Have fun.

Eat lots of fruit and vegetables and grains. Nutritionists recommend five servings of fruit and vegetables a day, but try to ignore that. I find as soon as nutritionists recommend something, I don't want to do it.

Remember that some of the best recipes

Regress with pleasure. Any food that reminds you of your childhood is okay in small doses, which is, of course, how you ate it when you were a child.

Don't forget to get your protein. Eggs, cheese, lean meats and fish, especially oily fish, are all grist for the mill.

Don't feel you have to peel everything.

Use more cold pressed oils which are high in monounsaturates.

Never apologise for your food.

Eat good bread.

Wash the dishes with a glad heart, the memory of the good food within you.

Have fun.

Use non-stick pans.

Remember to heat pans and woks before adding any oil, then you'll use less.

Remember that it is only food.

Drink a glass of good wine or mineral water instead of soft fizzy drink. Anything that has so many additives can't have had much to begin with.

If you must be obsessed with food, make sure it's good food.

Make your favourite recipe your own.

Don't garnish. Food is beautiful.

Taste everything. Think about how things taste, and why. Work out how you can make things taste better. Don't settle for the shock of sheer salt and sugar, or the temptation of crisp and crunchy, over true, real flavour. When we all learn to taste, there will be less fast food, more slow conversations, less war, more peace, fewer broken homes, more families sitting around tables, fewer morally loathsome films and TV soaps, and more honest work and creativity.

new food

It's time we changed the way we eat.

It's time we put together all that we have learned about good, fresh food, delicious flavours, healthy traditional diets, sustainable agriculture and new scientific knowledge, and came up with a **new way** of eating that our bodies, our lifestyles and our world can cope with.

I describe this **new food** as being part-Mediterranean, part-Asian, and part-cake because it bows to the past, sends kisses to Europe, shakes hands with Asia, and is **happy at home** in its own backyard.

Australia is slowly developing a style of cooking that **celebrates** everything we were, are and will be. This **new food** is a child born of both the traditional Mediterranean diet, and the equally ancient and healthy traditional Asian ways of eating.

By **Mediterranean**, I mean the use of olive oil, grains, pulses, fruits and vegetables, instead of butter, cream, processed foods, and red meats traditionally found in varying degrees throughout Greece, Italy, Spain, Turkey, Tunisia, Morocco, Portugal, southern France and parts of the Middle East. By **Asian**, I mean the insistence on freshness and seasonality, the simple use of fish, grains and vegetables, and the inspired

And where does cake fit in to all this, you ask? Wherever it can. Cake is a delicious reminder of our British heritage and a staple of our great country cooking. Australians have always known how to **do good cake**. The modern mantra of moderation just means we can appreciate it even more, while eating it a little less.

New food means having a steaming, spicy bowl of **curry laksa** for lunch one day and a Mediterranean **fish soup** the next, and never mixing the two.

It means cutting our dependence on animal fats, dairy products, starches and sugar, without beating ourselves up when we do **indulge**. It means wondering what grain to have for dinner tonight, instead of wondering what meat to choose. It means insisting on **quality** instead of quantity, and not putting up with mediocrity.

It means finding our own style of eating that makes us happy.

New scientific evidence suggests that our bodies are suffering because we are what we eat. Our diet is weakening our hearts and giving us cancer. At the same time, we are discovering that there is **less heart disease** and **less cancer** of the bowel and breast in Mediterranean countries, that Japan has one of the world's lowest rates of heart disease and the longest average life span, and that **cholesterol levels** are at a very healthy low in China. Since Mediterranean and Asian people started to move away from their traditional diets towards a Western one, however, they, too, are suffering.

We have the chance to learn from the past to safeguard our future, and to adjust our eating so that we **eat better** and **feel better** every day. It starts at home, as everything does. That's why most of the recipes are short and simple. Some recipes are long and simple for those with a whole weekend stretching out ahead of them and an understanding of **cooking as therapy**.

This book is proof that you can eat well, without fuss, pretension, or hard work. So choose yourself something to cook for dinner tonight, grab a glass of wine and head into that kitchen with a smile on your face. And don't ever feel scared, worried or intimidated by a recipe again.

Hell, it's only food. Just enjoy it.

new BREAKFASTS

The new breakfast is *organic, fresh, tangy,* and very, very necessary, for both body and soul. Life — and your stomach — would be empty without it.

Start the day with **muesli** or good old **porridge**, fresh **fruit** and live acidophilus **yoghurt**, some good, grainy **bread** that looks like birdseed, and a whole **apple**, not just juice. But do start the day with breakfast of some sort. The body sees it as fuel that will help keep it going all day, so haul it to the breakfast table and 'fill 'er up'. Without it, you are likely to run out of steam during the day, or worse, require some mechanical repair and panel-beating later in life.

Breakfast in its highest form is, of course, that taken lying down in bed. Just don't make it a big surprise. People don't like big surprises first thing in the morning. Besides, **breakfast in bed** is an extremely personal thing. It should only be shared by consenting adult couples whose relationships are established enough for them to have formed a few shared tastes.

The basic requirements are simple. **Fresh flowers**, newspapers, coffee, orange juice, bread, and, of course, that significant other who feels fresh enough to put it all together while you lie back and enjoy it.

If you have to do it yourself, keep the food simple and sweet and seductive. Try a **warm fruit** compote with spoonfuls of cream, grilled Italian pannetone bread flashed under the griller, warmed-through croissants sandwiched with prosciutto and bocconcini, and frothy pitchers of **freshly squeezed** orange or grapefruit juice, with just a swirl of Campari if it's late enough in the morning.

Or serve lazy layers of smoked salmon sleeping in on beds of toasted rye, quickly flipped pancakes (made with a dash of orange juice) topped with melting **lemon butter**, or creamy, dreamy omelettes folded over diced avocado and tomato.

Some mornings, of course, even a simple boiled egg served with soldiers of toast can be too much bother. In which case, just lie back and enjoy yourself. And go **out for lunch**.

french toast
with cinnamon
PHOTO 10-11
RECIPE 14

fresh apple
muesli
RECIPE 14

13

french **toast with cinnamon**

Sweet, cinnamon dusted bread in a batter spiked with orange juice makes a light, fresh and yummy way to start the day. The bread has to be at least a day old, or it will soften.

2 free range eggs

½ cup milk

½ teaspoon cinnamon

1 tablespoon orange juice

½ teaspoon cinnamon

2 teaspoons sugar

Fresh fruits in season

1 tablespoon butter

6 slices of day-old breadstick

1 orange, sliced, for garnish

beat eggs, milk, cinnamon and orange juice together to form a smooth batter.

mix remaining cinnamon and sugar, and prepare fruits.

melt butter in heavy based frypan.

dip each bread slice into batter, then straight into pan.

fry on both sides until golden, drain and place on warm plates.

pile fresh fruits on top, and sprinkle with cinnamon sugar.

serve with honey or maple syrup.

SERVES TWO

fresh **apple muesli**

Grated apple, yoghurt and honey-moistened rolled oats help my Swiss-born friend, chef Hermann Schneider face the day. He's right. It is almost worth getting out of bed for.

2 cups rolled oats

1 cup water

½ cup natural yoghurt

2 tablespoons honey

1 tablespoon wheatgerm

2 tablespoons freshly chopped nuts

1 banana, mashed

1 green apple, coarsely grated (with skin)

Any fruits or berries you like

soak rolled oats overnight in water.

add yoghurt, honey, wheatgerm, nuts, banana, apple and fruits.

top with more grated apple and serve.

SERVES FOUR

buckwheat **blinis with golden caviar**

A great way to have eggs for breakfast. Pile salmon caviar on these soft, yeasty blinis.

1 cup milk

15 grams (½ ounce) yeast

2 free range eggs, separated

Pinch of salt

Pinch of sugar

2 tablespoons melted butter

1½ cups buckwheat flour, sifted

2 tablespoons fresh salmon caviar

1 cup crème fraîche

bring milk to boil, cool until barely warm, and whisk in the yeast.

leave for 30 minutes.

beat egg yolks until thick.

add milk and yeast, salt, sugar, butter and flour and mix well.

beat egg whites until stiff, then fold gently into batter.

lightly butter a small frypan pan and heat.

spoon in enough batter to form an 8 cm (3 in) crêpe, and cook for about 30 seconds on either side until golden.

repeat until batter is finished.

trim edges of blini and top with crème fraîche and caviar.

serve warm or at room temperature.

MAKES TEN OR TWELVE

yoghurt **fruit smoothie**

The laziest breakfast in the world; no chopping, no peeling, no slicing, and no dirty dishes. It's fast, healthy food you can drink.

2 cups fruit (berries, melon, banana)

1 cup natural yoghurt

2 tablespoons honey

1 cup crushed ice

½ cup orange juice

whizz.

if you want it thicker, add more banana.

if you want it thinner, add more orange juice.

if you want it prettier, add more berries.

if you want it easier, forget it. It doesn't get any easier than this.

SERVES TWO

champagne sausages with spiced apples

A great breakfast, brunch, or — if you really sleep in — lunch. Use this poaching technique with any good sausage to add flavour.

6 chicken sausages

1 cup champagne

2 tablespoons butter

2 green apples, peeled and sliced

½ teaspoon cinnamon

1 tablespoon brown sugar

prick sausages, place in champagne in a frypan and bring to boil.

reduce to a simmer and cook for 10 minutes.

drain, slash sausage sides with a knife, and quickly grill or pan fry until brown.

melt butter in a frypan, add apples and cook for 3 minutes.

add cinnamon and sugar, toss to coat, and cook over a low heat until apples have softened and turned golden brown.

serve with sausages and potato pancakes.

SERVES TWO

shredded potato pancake

Serve with champagne sausages and spiced apples as shown here, or with poached eggs and bacon, or smoked salmon and cream cheese.

3 red skinned potatoes

1 tablespoon grated onion

1 free range egg, beaten

Pinch of salt

3 tablespoons vegetable oil

peel and grate potatoes.

add onion.

mix egg with salt and 1 tablespoon of oil, and stir into potato mixture.

let stand for a few minutes, then squeeze out excess moisture with your hands.

heat remaining oil in small frypan. When hot but not smoking, drop in a heaped tablespoon of potato, and squash it flat until it is roughly 10 cm (4 in) in diameter.

fry on both sides until golden brown.

drain on paper towel and serve hot.

MAKES FOUR

champagne
sausages with
spiced apples
and shredded
potato pancake

golden **popovers**

The secret with these light little buns is to combine the ingredients with a light hand, and to not overmix. They are best eaten straight from the pan, served with berry jam and a triple cream cheese such as Brillat-Savarin, St André or an Australian Jindi.

2 free range eggs

1 cup plain flour, sifted

½ teaspoon salt

1 cup milk

2 tablespoons melted butter

beat eggs lightly and beat in flour and salt.
stir in milk, and blend to a smooth batter.
add melted butter and pour into a buttered muffin tray or patty pan, filling only to two-thirds.
place in a cold oven, set oven to 200°C (400°F), and bake for 25 to 30 minutes until golden brown.
don't open oven door during baking or they may traumatise and fall.

MAKES SIX

mexican **eggs with tortillas and chilli sauce**

The ultimate breakfast in Mexico — fried eggs on corn tortillas with a country-style chilli sauce. It also makes a great lunch or supper, so don't worry if you sleep in.

6 ripe tomatoes

2 fresh red chillies

2 garlic cloves, peeled

2 tablespoons peanut oil

4 small tortillas (see New Basics, page 216)

4 free range eggs

Coriander leaves

1 avocado

1 red capsicum

1 tomato

bake whole tomatoes, chillies and garlic at 160°C (325°F) for one hour, turning occasionally, until tomatoes soften and skin starts to colour and peel.
blend, seeds and all, in a food processor until smooth, and set aside.
heat oil in a frypan and fry tortillas quickly on both sides.
drain on paper towel and keep warm, covered, while cooking the eggs. The tortilla should be soft, not crisp.
break eggs into the same oil and cook to your liking.
heat sauce, place one egg on each tortilla, and cover or circle with sauce.
sprinkle with coriander leaves, and add sliced avocado, capsicum, or tomatoes as you please.

SERVES TWO

scrambled **eggs wrapped in smoked salmon**

An impressive breakfast that takes one minute to cook but looks as if you've been up all night getting it to look so good. (People love that.)

2 slices of smoked salmon per person

6 free range eggs

1 tablespoon chives, chopped

Sea salt and freshly ground pepper

1 teaspoon butter

4 wholegrain muffins

A few mixed green leaves

1 tablespoon walnut or hazelnut oil

1 tablespoon of your best vinegar

line 4 small moulds with the salmon, leaving some hanging over the edge.

break eggs into a bowl.

add chives, a dash of water, salt and pepper, and break up with a fork.

melt butter in a heavy bottomed saucepan and scramble eggs over a light heat, stirring and scraping constantly with a wooden spoon.

spoon into the salmon-lined moulds and fold remaining salmon over top to cover.

turn each mould upside down onto a grilled, halved muffin.

dress salad greens, and arrange on other halves.

serve quick-smart.

SERVES FOUR

moroccan **figs with fresh pears and yoghurt**

Sweet and spicy pears and dried fruits that can be done a day or two ahead and stored in syrup in the fridge.

1 cup dried figs

1 bottle light red wine (pinot noir or rosé)

2 cups water

1 cup sugar

3 cinnamon sticks, broken

10 cloves

10 peppercorns

1 vanilla bean, split lengthwise

Rind of 1 lemon, cut into thin strips

1 cup dried apricots

1 cup raisins

6 pears, peeled

1 cup natural yoghurt

soak figs in water for a few hours, then drain.

combine wine, water, sugar, cinnamon, cloves, peppercorns, vanilla bean, and lemon rind and simmer for 10 minutes.

add dried fruits and simmer for 15 minutes.

remove fruits with slotted spoon, add pears and poach gently for 8 minutes or until cooked but still firm.

return all fruits to syrup and allow to cool.

serve at room temperature or chilled, with a bowl of natural yoghurt.

SERVES SIX

egg **and bacon pizza**

Yes, eggs and bacon, on an edible plate. If you really want to sleep in, use ready-made pizza bases, although this dough is a cinch.

50 grams (2 ounces) butter

350 grams (12 ounces) self-raising flour

1 teaspoon lemon juice

1 cup milk

1 tablespoon tomato paste

4 rashers bacon

1 tomato, sliced

2 free range eggs

1 tablespoon olive oil

preheat oven to 200°C (400°F).

cut butter into cubes, and place in food processor with flour.

stop and start the machine until mixture resembles fine breadcrumbs.

add lemon juice and milk and stop-start until a ball forms.

turn dough onto floured board and knead lightly, then halve.

roll out each half and cut into 15 cm (6 in) diameter circles.

pinch edges slightly, and brush base with tomato paste.

grill or fry bacon and drain.

place bacon and tomato on each pizza, and carefully break an egg into each centre.

drizzle with a little olive oil and bake for 10 minutes.

egg and bacon pizza

Global changes in our eating habits over the last decade before the twenty-first century have cooked up a whole new language.

Trying too hard

The most common mistake of late 'eighties and early 'nineties dinner parties. 'Poor Emma, she tried too hard.' Next time, she must try harder in order to make everything appear relaxed and spontaneous.

OP's

Overprocessed, overpackaged, overpriced foods, designed for people who spend a lot of time and money trying to save themselves time and money.

Doily cuisine

A derogatory term given to old-fashioned, over-garnished (often hotel) food.

Fake food

Food that is artificially coloured and flavoured to look like real food, but there is nothing genuine about it except for the desire by the manufacturer to produce as many as possible for as little as possible.

Crépinetting

The interaction between food writers, restaurant reviewers, produce suppliers and chefs that is considered essential by all concerned in order to promote themselves.

Remote control cuisine

Food that is bought, cooked and eaten automatically, without thought given to quality or taste.

Ethnic surfing

Culinary promiscuity, or the embracing of a national multicultural identity. Also known as (con)fusion cooking. You know: east meets west, Middle East meets west, north meets south, nor nor east meets sou sou west, that sort of thing. The food, generally, gets lost in the middle. Prime examples: Thai burritos, Greek wontons, Chinese fajitas, Mexican tirami su. (Actual recipes in San Francisco *Examiner*, July, 1993).

The permanent tomato

A product of genetic engineering, the Flavr-Savr tomato was recently launched in America. May the concept rot as quietly and naturally as a fresh tomato.

Smorgasbored

(also known by the acronym AYCE)

A medical condition linked to the attendance of

new food language

Zapping

This used to refer to the practice of fast-forwarding through commercial breaks on the television. Now, it means fast-forwarding through commercial food in the microwave.

Marco Pierrism

The mimicking of the infamous Marco Pierre White of the famous London restaurant, Harvey's, whose dishes are themselves (accredited) mimics of Pierre Koffman, Albert Roux and Nico Ladenis creations.

Recipism

The tendency to follow a recipe to the letter, frequently ending on step five of a nine-step process when you suddenly realise you have no dried

Conspicuous consumption

Eating outdoors.

SDT

The sun-dried tomato, a preserved fruit that was never intended, by those who dried the first tomato, to be added to everything.

Restaurantitis

A phenomenon that occurs when a group of friends choose the restaurant for the quality of its food, only to ignore said food when it arrives, in favour of talking about other restaurants they

new BRUNCHES

eggplant,
tomato and

Sunday was only invented so that one could brunch. When breakfast is too early and lunch is too late, brunch is the only **civilised thing** to do. It is also a very cool, casual and cost-effective way to entertain.

Tell everyone to come at noon, and to bring the newspapers with them. That way, you have Saturday in which to shop, cook and clean, and by Sunday morning you can just get up and set the table. If that's still too hard, just close all the doors to the messy rooms and open the door to the courtyard, backyard or balcony for instant atmosphere.

Brunch should have a buffet air, with a spread that stretches as far as the budget. It should also be as **simple** as possible. Rather than lots of little things, concentrate on a few **very generous** things. Chill bottles of champagne in buckets of ice, pile oven-warmed rolls in cloth-lined baskets, and open **every jar of jam** in the house. Have Twinings English Breakfast or herbal tea and **great coffee** on standby all day.

Brunch can be as simple as foaming glasses of Guinness teamed with freshly opened oysters and spicy pork sausages, or as complex as a ten-course Cantonese yum cha. You can poach a whole Atlantic salmon or ocean trout, or lay out platters of prosciutto, mortadella and juicy slices of melon.

And when in doubt, **add champagne**. Pour it into icy cold flutes and over huge glass bowls of fruit salad. Poach sausages in it (yes, it's **fabulous!**), drizzle it over tiny strawberries nestled into halved melons, and into the juice of oranges, mixed with a little strawberry liqueur.

Above all, **relax**. Forget the formal dining room. Set up a big table in the kitchen or on the balcony or verandah instead. Let the dogs and kids out, turn up the radio, put up your feet, and pour another glass of champagne. If at least one of your guests is missing halfway through the afternoon, only to be discovered curled up under the lemon tree snoring peacefully, brunch has been an unqualified success. You'll never

champagne **ice-cream sodas**

The coolest way to start the day. Buy lemon gelato from your favourite Italian gelateria, and keep champagne and glasses well chilled.

Lemon gelato (allow 3 small scoops per person)

Champagne

scoop 2 or 3 scoops of gelato into each champagne flute.

pour champagne over gelato very slowly, allowing it to froth up a little.

use straws and parfait spoons if you like, although it's just as much fun to sip it as the lemon gelato melts and forms what is, in effect, a champagne spider.

steamed crab sui mai
RECIPE 30
and champagne ice-cream sodas

grilled **polenta with gorgonzola**

A revered antipasto at the Bottega del Vino in Verona in northern Italy, where it has been served since 1890. Over one hundred years later, it is still exciting and new. Make the polenta the day before, so that all you have to do is grill it.

1 quantity polenta (see New Basics, page 211)

1 tablespoon olive oil

100 grams (4 ounces) Italian gorgonzola
or equivalent creamy blue cheese

cut polenta into 2.5 cm (1 in) squares and brush tops and bottoms with a little oil.

grill until one side is golden, then turn and grill other side.

top immediately with squares of gorgonzola cheese, so that it melts down the sides. These are also wonderful topped with prosciutto, spoonfuls of sweet, slow-cooked onions, or strips of roasted red peppers.

SERVES FOUR

grilled polenta
with gorgonzola

steamed **crab sui mai**

Grab the ingredients from an Asian food store, and make these sophisticated, bite-size dumplings beforehand, ready to steam and serve.

450 grams (1 pound) green prawns

1 cup fresh or canned crab meat

250 grams (9 ounces) minced pork

2 tablespoons water chestnuts, finely chopped

2 tablespoons bamboo shoot, finely chopped

2 tablespoons spring onion, chopped

1 tablespoon grated ginger

1 tablespoon light soy sauce

1 tablespoon Chinese rice wine or dry sherry

1 egg white

1 packet of wonton pastry skins

2 tablespoons green peas

peel and devein prawns and chop finely.

mix with crab, minced pork, water chestnuts, bamboo shoot, spring onion, ginger, soy sauce, rice wine and egg white until mixture is a homogeneous paste.

dob a teaspoonful of mixture onto each wonton skin, gently gather up the sides and press gently to form a pouch.

top each with a green pea, place on a sheet of greaseproof paper and steam for 20 minutes.

serve with soy sauce.

MAKES TWENTY

fresh **vietnamese spring rolls**

These are the lightest, tangiest, healthiest spring rolls around, wrapped in almost transparent rice paper rounds that have been dunked in boiling water. Try filling with grilled chicken, scallops, and lightly steamed vegetables.

1 packet of dried rice paper rounds

1 cup rice vermicelli

12 small prawns, cooked and peeled

Shredded iceberg lettuce

3 tablespoons fresh bean shoots

2 tablespoons beer nuts

Bunch of fresh mint

Bunch of fresh coriander

toss noodles into boiling water for 5 minutes or until tender.

drain and rinse in cold water.

dunk each rice paper round into boiling water for a few seconds until soft, and spread out to drain on serving plates.

place on each paper some shredded lettuce, noodles, beanshoots, nuts, mint and coriander, and fold the rice paper towards the centre to form a firm roll.

tuck in 3 small prawns, fold in ends of rice paper, and roll into a neat sausage shape. Rice paper will stick to itself and hold the shape. Dip into nuoc cham sauce (see New Basics, page 214).

SERVES FOUR

warm **fig salad with prosciutto**

A heavenly combination of sweet, warm seedy figs and salty prosciutto. A dollop of mascarpone and some grilled bread slicked with garlicky olive oil, and you can die happy.

12 ripe purple-skinned figs

1 garlic clove

Extra virgin olive oil

Crusty bread

12 slices of prosciutto

6 dessertspoons mascarpone

cut an X into the top of each fig, wrap loosely in foil, and bake in a 160°C (325°F) oven for 10 to 15 minutes to warm through.

smash garlic clove and leave to infuse in a small dish of olive oil.

grill bread until golden, then brush lightly with olive oil.

unwrap figs from foil, then wrap each one in a slice of prosciutto.

pour any juices over the top, then top with mascarpone and serve with grilled bread.

SERVES SIX

champagne **crêpes with strawberries**

A stack of champagne-flavoured crêpes sandwiched with fresh strawberries and cream that will keep you brunching all day.

5 free range eggs

1 tablespoon sugar

1½ cups champagne

1 tablespoon melted butter

140 grams (5 ounces) plain flour

Pinch of salt

2 tablespoons butter for cooking

3 punnets small strawberries

1 cup whipping cream

1 tablespoon strawberry liqueur

Fresh mint

blend eggs, sugar, champagne, butter, flour and salt in blender. Strain, and leave to rest for an hour.

heat a touch of the butter in a 15 cm (6 in) pan.

pour in just enough batter to cover bottom, tilting to make it spread.

cook gently until air bubbles appear, then turn crêpe and cook until golden.

remove, wipe pan clean with paper towel, add a touch more butter, and repeat process, layering crêpes with waxed paper until you have at least 10.

whip cream, add strawberry liqueur, and spread on one crêpe, top with strawberries and mint, add another crêpe, and continue.

cover and chill.

to serve, cut as if slicing a cake.

SERVES SIX

fresh **oysters with avocado, tomato and lime**

Loosen the oysters on the shell so that you can lift them to your mouth and slide them in. Add a dash of vodka or Tabasco sauce if everyone needs waking up.

2 dozen oysters, freshly opened

Salad greens

1 avocado

Juice of 2 limes or lemons

2 tomatoes

1 tablespoon snipped chives

arrange oysters on a bed of salad greens.

peel avocado, chop into small dice, and sprinkle with lime or lemon juice.

dunk tomatoes in a pot of boiling water for a few seconds, remove, and peel.

cut tomatoes in half, gently squeeze out the seeds, then chop remaining flesh into small dice.

combine avocado and tomato with chives and remaining juice, and spoon over oysters in shells.

SERVES SIX

champagne
crêpes with
strawberries
RECIPE 31

fresh oysters
with avocado,
tomato and
lime

vodka **scrambled eggs with gravlax**

The ultimate thick, soft, creamy scrambled eggs touched with vodka, teamed with dill-cured salmon gravlax from the deli, and grilled sourdough bread.

1 tablespoon butter

1 garlic clove

10 free range eggs

2 tablespoons vodka

2 tablespoons sour cream

6 slices of crusty sourdough bread

6 generous slices of gravlax

melt butter in a heavy bottomed saucepan sitting in a pan of simmering water on top of the stove.

peel garlic, and spear with a fork. Use fork to lightly beat eggs in a bowl, then discard garlic.

add vodka and sour cream.

pour eggs into saucepan, and cook slowly, gently stirring with a wooden spoon until mixture thickens. The slower it cooks, the creamier it will be.

grill or toast bread, and warm plates.

pour eggs over bread, and serve with slices of salmon.

SERVES SIX

lime **scallops with avocado**

The lime juice virtually cooks the seafood before you toss it with coconut milk and avocado. Marinate seafood the night before so there is little to do on the day.

6 scallops per person

4 small squid tubes, cleaned

½ cup lime juice

1 cup canned coconut milk

Fresh basil

1 avocado

1 tablespoon lemon juice

8 red cherry tomatoes, halved

8 yellow pear tomatoes, halved

wash and dry scallops, and remove brown intestinal tracts.

slice squid tubes into thin rings.

marinate scallops and squid in lime juice for at least 3 hours, tossing occasionally.

add coconut milk and gently mix.

peel avocado, cut into cubes, and sprinkle cubes with lemon juice.

tear basil into strips.

drain scallops and squid, and gently toss with avocado, tomatoes and basil.

serve with corn chips.

SERVES FOUR

eggplant, **tomato and white cheese stack**

A delicious brunch, lunch or light snack, these stacks are just as happy partnering grilled lamb or chicken.

2 medium eggplants

Salt

Olive oil

5 large tomatoes

300 grams (11 ounces) fresh ricotta cheese

Freshly ground pepper

A few basil leaves

slice eggplant, salt, and leave for 1 hour.

rinse, wipe dry, and brush with oil.

slice tomatoes thickly, and brush with oil.

grill eggplant until golden brown.

lay a slice of eggplant on serving plate, top with ricotta and a few twists of pepper.

add a slice of tomato, then top with eggplant.

brush sides of stack with a little olive oil and bake at 200°C (400°F) for 10 minutes.

tuck basil leaves in stacks and serve warm or cold.

SERVES FOUR

focaccia **with sweet onion marmalade**

Sweet onions turn focaccia into a dreamy, fragrant pizza. If bread is quite thick, slice it in half before topping with onions and herbs.

1 cup sweet onion marmalade (see New Basics, page 214)

1 large focaccia (Italian flatbread)

2 tablespoons fresh rosemary sprigs

1 tablespoon brown sugar

spread onion marmalade over focaccia, and sprinkle with rosemary and sugar.

bake in a 200°C (400°F) oven, or grill for 5 to 10 minutes until hot and starting to crisp.

cut into small squares and serve.

MAKES SIXTEEN

Olive oil is the lifeblood of the Mediterranean. It has given light, flavour and good health for centuries. The noble olive tree has given shelter, warmth and food. Olive oil, says Lawrence Durrell, is 'a taste older than meat, older than wine. A taste as old as cold water'.

Olive oil is an entirely natural product that contains more monounsaturated fatty acids than any other fat or oil. The good oil on olive oil is that it can reduce the 'bad' cholesterol in the bloodstream while raising the 'good', protective cholesterol. Indeed, the latest research suggests it is even more vital because its generous amount of anti-oxidants, like those of fruits and vegetables, can help prevent the bad cholesterol from oxidising.

According to the International Olive Oil Council, whose members set the worldwide standards for olive oils, these are the types available:

extra virgin olive oil Top shelf olive oil, of absolutely perfect taste and colour, with an intense fruity flavour and a maximum acidity (in terms of oleic free fatty acid) of 1%.

virgin olive oil Excellent fruit flavour and a maximum acidity of 3%.

olive oil A blend of refined or purified olive oil, blended with virgin olive oil to give it more flavour.

light and extra light olive oils are blends of refined olive oil and small amounts of virgin olive oil, and are lighter in flavour (though not in kilojoules).

The best flavour comes from extra virgin olive oil. Use it for everything if you can afford it, and move down the scale reluctantly.

The better the flavour of your oil, the less you need to use. Certainly, use your very best oils for your simplest dishes, on the basis of quality over quantity. Extra virgin olive oil is wonderful when drizzled over grilled country style bread or over a bowl of cooked white beans and rosemary. Adding it unheated to food as it is served also preserves its vital anti-oxidants.

Olive oils should be stored in a cool place (not on top of the refrigerator or near the stove). Their flavour will deteriorate after twelve months, so it is best to buy smaller quantities of different types than it is to buy in a bulk quantity that you may not use.

Like grapes, olives differ in flavour from place to place. In Italy, the late-harvested Ligurian oils are the sweetest and most delicate, with intense olive flavour and low acidity, while Tuscan oil is fruity, green and as rich as the richest Florentine. Olive oils from Apulia and Calabria in southern Italy have more of a peppery bite, while in France, Provençal oil is a dark olive green with a mild fruity bouquet. Olive trees are now grown commercially in Australia and are producing some good, pale and mildly fruity olive oils. Look for oils from Toscana in Central Victoria, and from inspired winemakers in South Australia like Joe Grilli of Primo Estate and Mark and Anne Lloyd of McLaren Vale.

olive

OIL

the little black

D R E S

Trust Modena, the most elegant city in Italy, to be the home of balsamic vinegar. Here, the ancient homes have high-ceilinged attics devoted to its production, a long, slow process traditionally tended by the women of the house.

Each noble Modenese family made their own vinegar, from mainly white Trebbiano grapes, for the next generation. It became a dowry more valuable than gold and jewels, to send with a proud daughter to her new home. For hundreds of years, it was prized as a soothing and healing balsam, its sweetness, sourness and strength was likened to a fine perfume or an aged sherry.

While many families still keep their balsamic vinegar as a private pleasure, there are now more public producers like the Giusti family, who have been making their balsamic vinegar (Aceto Balsamico di Giuseppe Giusti) in the same attic, and in the same barrels since 1605.

First, the grapes are boiled down to a thick, sweet syrup in copper barrels. The mother vinegar is added, and the vinegar begins its long, slow journey from cask to cask, from oak to chestnut to mulberry to juniper and cherrywood, each ancient wood imparting its own fragrance, colour and complexity to the liqueur.

Signor Giusti says that only by using the choicest grapes, the traditional seasoning, the small, ancient wooden barrels and the wisdom born of experience can he give the vinegar its special characteristic flavour.

Balsamic vinegar is aged for twenty years before it is bottled for sale. Some are aged for forty, eighty and even one hundred years. Yet it takes just a few seconds to add its magical complexity to our food.

20 things to do with balsamic vinegar

dash a little balsamic vinegar over grilled sardines instead of lemon juice.

intensify the sweetness of strawberries by tossing them first in a little sugar, then in balsamic vinegar. The effect is extraordinary.

sprinkle balsamic vinegar over chargrilled or roasted lamb.

add a splash to your risotto and stir through just before serving.

splash onto some grilled pork sausages just before serving.

for a warm salad of chicken livers, heat a little olive oil, add cleaned and chopped chicken livers and toss quickly. At the last moment add a tablespoon or two of balsamic vinegar, then tip the whole lot onto curly endive greens (frisée).

splash a teaspoonful of balsamic vinegar into a clear chicken soup.

make a spicy green sauce (salsa verde) by chopping two hard-boiled eggs with lots of parsley, basil, some capers, anchovies, freshly ground pepper, olive oil and balsamic vinegar. Serve spooned over poached veal tongue, corned beef, grilled sausages or your favourite meats.

moisten torn country style bread with water and squeeze dry. Toss it with balsamic vinegar, extra virgin olive oil, torn basil and sliced raw tomato and leave for two hours to infuse.

dissolve a little sugar in balsamic vinegar, add crushed ice and mineral water.

splash croutons with balsamic vinegar and toast in a hot oven until crisp. Throw them into a green salad with a softly poached egg.

fill the gentle curve of a fresh ripe avocado with a little balsamic vinegar, extra virgin olive oil and freshly ground pepper.

use it instead of lemon juice in your homemade mayonnaise.

gently sauté chicken pieces in olive oil, garlic and sage, then add a tablespoon or two of balsamic vinegar towards the end of the cooking time to flavour the juices.

drizzle a spoonful over hot boiled baby beetroots and top with snipped chives.

add a chic splash to jewel-coloured roasted vegetables.

sprinkle a teaspoonful of balsamic vinegar over a warm herb omelette or Italian frittata.

slice small zucchini very, very thinly and fry quickly in olive oil. Transfer immediately to a platter, douse with balsamic vinegar, and toss with salt, sugar, black pepper and freshly torn mint.

peel long thin shavings of fine parmigiano reggiano with a vegetable peeler, pile into a pyramid with shavings of crisp celery, and sprinkle balsamic vinegar over all.

at its very simplest, toss a tablespoon of balsamic vinegar over a sliced ripe tomato, leave for an hour, and do nothing else at all except eat it.

SING

new LUNCHES

roasted
eggplant with
goat's cheese
and thyme
RECIPE 46

'Let's have lunch'

are the three words that will save the human race. To invite someone to lunch is a great statement of **friendship**. To give lunch in your own home means emerging from your carefully constructed cocoons of answering machines, computer games and exercise bicycles long enough to sit at a table with people you care about. It means a few bottles of **wine** and hours of **talking** about nothing (or was it something?), and getting to know the **people** in your life a little better.

Lunch has a fresh **rosiness** to it, with all the promise of the endless afternoon ahead, and all the joy of family and friends and cats and dogs and the ensuing disaster around you.

If you think lunch at home is simply a dinner party in daylight, you've got it all wrong. It is crucial that the food you serve at lunch be Lunch Food. Eggs benedict is breakfast. Boeuf Bourguignon is dinner. Lunch is **antipasto, yum cha, mezes** and **tapas**. It can be as high-powered or as low key as you like. **Pizza** is great for lunch, a plain roasted chicken superb, fish and shellfish ideal.

A new favourite for lunch is a fragrant **Vietnamese chicken soup** with velvety rice noodles, to which each person adds tangy fish sauce, lemon juice, chilli and peppery Asian mint. It seems to go particularly well with champagne.

Fresh fruit and **cheese** are the best way to finish, neck and neck with coffee and a slice of **richly iced cake**.

Lunch should appear spontaneous and impromptu, even if invitations went out three weeks ago. Lunch was meant to be **easy**. Skip starters and launch straight into it. Get the kids fed so they can go and destroy the garden. Encourage those left to pour their own wine and help themselves to food. This can be done very simply by refusing to serve them anything yourself.

A garden setting, a fruit-laden table, jugs of wine, sourdough breads and whole rounds of cheese. **That's lunch**. And it should by rights continue until dinner, when you kick everyone out and crawl back into your cocoon with the leftovers and the last glass of bubbly.

pasta with
olives, lemon
and ham
RECIPE 45

vineyard **sausages with grapes**

The original salsiccie all'uva, as shown in
Recipes from an Italian Farmhouse *by*
Valentina Harris is rich and oily, with sausage
fat mingling with the sweet grapes. By grilling
the sausages first, you can limit your fat intake
and still get plenty of flavour.

12 Italian pork sausages

1 kilo (2 pounds) firm, ripe green grapes

2 tablespoons dry white wine

Flat-leaf parsley

wash and dry grapes, leaving them in small bunches.

prick sausages well, and grill over high heat until firm and golden brown.

place in a frypan with grapes and wine, and heat.

toss gently as the wine evaporates, the grapes heat, and their juices mingle with any sausage juices.

pile sausages onto serving plate and top with warmed grapes, grape juices from pan, and parsley.

SERVES FOUR TO SIX

pasta **with olives, lemon and ham**

A dead-easy dish with lots of colour and lots of
flavour. Serve it hot on the spot, or let it cool
and pretend you have invented a new form of
pasta salad.

2 tablespoons lemon juice

3 tablespoons virgin olive oil

8 slices of prosciutto

2 tablespoons small black olives

2 teaspoons fresh thyme

Grated rind of 2 lemons

Freshly ground pepper

100 grams (4 ounces) spaghetti per person

mix lemon juice and olive oil in a big bowl.

cut prosciutto into thin strips and toss with olives, thyme, lemon rind, and pepper.

cook pasta in plenty of boiling, salted water until tender, but firm to the bite (around 8 to 10 minutes).

drain and toss with prosciutto and olives.

pour on enough of the dressing to coat, toss gently and serve.

SERVES FOUR

drunken chicken

A classic Cantonese recipe from my friend Elizabeth Chong. The tender meat is imbued with aromatic Chinese shao hsing wine, giving it an almost mystical fragrance and flavour.

1 small fresh free range chicken

1 ½ teaspoons salt

2 teaspoons sugar

1 cup shao hsing rice wine

rub chicken with salt and sugar, inside and out and leave for an hour.

pour wine over chicken, inside and out, and leave for another 7 hours, turning a few times.

steam chicken in its dish of wine for 15 minutes only.

cool.

chop the chicken in the Chinese way: use a cleaver to halve the bird along the breast-bone. Cut wings and drumsticks away from breast, then chop each joint and each breast into three.

serve chicken at room temperature, drizzled with wine marinade.

SERVES EIGHT

roasted eggplant with goat's cheese and thyme

Smoky eggplant, tangy goat's cheese, and sweet thyme meet and mingle on crisp crostini to make Mediterranean magic. Try to find the freshest, tangiest goat's cheese, like Gabrielle Kervella's beautiful Fromage Fermier from Western Australia.

4 eggplants

1 tablespoon virgin olive oil

1 teaspoon ground cumin

Salt and freshly ground pepper

1 loaf of country style bread

200 grams (7 ounces) goat's cheese

1 tablespoon walnut oil

Sprigs of fresh thyme

Mixed salad greens

wash and dry eggplants, drizzle with olive oil, and bake at 200°C (400°F) for 30 minutes until skin darkens.

cool, peel, and squeeze any bitter juices out of the flesh.

bung into food processor with cumin, salt and pepper, and process to a rough paste.

slice bread, and cut 3 rounds of bread per person with a cookie cutter.

bake for 10 minutes at 200°C (400°F) until golden.

top each crostini with eggplant paste and crumbled goat's cheese.

drizzle with walnut oil, then grill until cheese melts.

serve on salad greens, topped with thyme.

SERVES FOUR

vietnamese **stuffed calamari**

You can stuff the calamari ahead of time, then bake or barbecue in an instant, for easy entertaining. Try to find small calamari tubes for this dish.

6 dried Chinese mushrooms

1 cup thin cellophane noodles (bean thread)

6 small calamari, cleaned

1 tablespoon peanut oil

2 shallots or spring onions, chopped

250 grams (9 ounces) minced pork or chicken

1 garlic clove, chopped

2 tablespoons fish sauce (nam pla)

Pinch of sugar

Freshly ground pepper

1 tablespoon fresh coriander, chopped

1 tablespoon lemon juice

1 tablespoon peanut oil

soak mushrooms in warm water for 30 minutes, then drain and chop.

pour boiling water over noodles and leave for 20 minutes, then drain and rinse.

heat oil in a wok and stir fry shallots, meat and garlic.

add mushrooms, noodles, fish sauce, sugar, pepper, coriander and lemon juice.

stuff calamari tubes until two-thirds full, and close ends with satay sticks.

baste with oil, prick twice, and bake at 200°C (400°F) or grill, for 5 minutes.

slice and serve.

SERVES SIX

warm **prawn and mint salad**

A quick and easy dish, alive with the fresh tang of mint and chilli. Substitute lobster tails if you're feeling extravagant.

12 green (raw) prawns

1 tablespoon fish sauce (nam pla)

Juice of 1 lime or lemon

3 tablespoons coconut milk

1 teaspoon sugar

1 garlic clove, crushed

1 teaspoon grated fresh ginger

2 fresh red chillies, finely sliced

Freshly ground pepper

2 tablespoons fresh mint leaves

peel prawns, leaving tail, and devein by hooking out the intestinal tract with a fine skewer or satay stick.

drop prawns into simmering, salted water for a minute or two until they turn pink.

mix fish sauce, lime juice, coconut milk, sugar, garlic, ginger, chillies and pepper.

toss prawns in dressing, add mint leaves and mix.

SERVES FOUR

baby **calamari with anchovy and basil**

Go for the small whole calamari, even if you have to clean them out yourself. They're cheaper, fresher, and much nicer than the large orthopaedic tubes.

450 grams (1 pound) squid tubes

3 tablespoons virgin olive oil

4 anchovies, rinsed and dried

2 garlic cloves, finely minced

Freshly ground pepper

3 tablespoons flat-leaf parsley, chopped

4 teaspoons pesto (see New Basics, page 210)

if you buy the whole squid, separate the head and tentacles from the body, and discard the head.

if you buy the headless white tubes, just clean and rinse them. Cut any tentacles in half, and the body into ringlets.

warm olive oil, and add anchovy and garlic.

stir, breaking up the anchovy, until garlic starts to sizzle.

raise the heat, add squid, and cook, tossing squid quickly until it turns opaque, which will take only 1 or 2 minutes.

spoon onto warm serving plates, piling high, and top with a dollop of pesto.

SERVES FOUR

grilled **focaccia with everything**

Soft and crusty at the same time, focaccia lends itself generously to done-on-the-run summer lunches. If family and friends are in and out all day, just leave 'the makings', and they can fix their own.

3 red capsicums

Focaccia

6 thin slices of good tasty cheese

6 slices of prosciutto

2 tablespoons pesto (see New Basics, page 210)

2 tablespoons sun-dried tomato paste

6 artichoke hearts, preserved in oil

1 tablespoon tiny capers, rinsed

place capsicums in 200°C (400°F) oven and bake for 30 minutes until skin blisters and darkens.

place in a covered bowl for 10 minutes, then peel, discarding juice and seeds.

cut focaccia into 6 segments, and cut open each 'bun'.

lay a slice of cheese and prosciutto on one half, and assemble artichoke hearts, roasted capsicum, capers, pesto and sun-dried tomato paste on the other.

grill each side until cheese melts, then join halves and grill the top very quickly. Tuck in a fresh basil leaf and serve.

SERVES SIX

grilled foccacia
with everything

prosciutto with sweet and sour melon

Balsamic vinegar accentuates the sweetness of the melon, while the prosciutto adds a salty contrast. Serve with a chilled wine aperitif while sitting in the sun.

1 ripe canteloupe

10 thin slices of prosciutto

2 tablespoons balsamic vinegar

10 wooden satay sticks

Freshly ground pepper

peel and seed canteloupe and cut into nice chunky cubes.

toss cubes in balsamic vinegar and set aside for an hour or so.

thread the end of a slice of prosciutto on a satay stick.

add a cube of melon, then thread the prosciutto back onto the skewer.

add more melon and continue process until each skewer has prosciutto snaking in and out of the melon chunks.

twist pepper over each stick and serve.

SERVES TEN

chargrilled vegetables with extra virgin olive oil

A madly Mediterranean mélange of colourful vegetables flashed under the grill or on the barbecue for an easy lunch.

1 garlic clove, smashed

Extra virgin olive oil

Salt and freshly ground pepper

3 baby eggplants

3 yellow zucchini

3 green zucchini

6 spring onions

1 red capsicum

1 green capsicum

Fresh sage

Fresh rosemary

swirl garlic through olive oil, and season with salt and pepper.

slice eggplants and zucchini.

trim spring onions.

deseed capsicums and cut into 4.

brush everything with a little of the garlicky olive oil, and grill until vegetables darken and their skins start to blister.

pile all vegetables together on plates, drizzle with a touch more olive oil, and tuck in sprigs of sage and rosemary.

SERVES FOUR

chargrilled vegetables with extra virgin olive oil

salmon niçois

Southern France's best salad, dressed up with Australia's wonderful Atlantic salmon. Serve with crusty French bread and an Australian sauvignon blanc.

6 small fillets Atlantic salmon

1 tablespoon olive oil for cooking

2 tablespoons red wine vinegar

2 tablespoons extra virgin olive oil

1 teaspoon Dijon mustard

Salt and freshly ground pepper

6 small red-skinned potatoes, cooked

250 grams (9 ounces) green beans, lightly cooked

6 plum tomatoes, quartered

1 continental cucumber, peeled and finely sliced

2 green capsicums, cored and deseeded

4 spring onions, thinly sliced

8 anchovy fillets

3 hard-boiled eggs, quartered

2 tablespoons small black olives

remove skin from salmon.

heat a little olive oil in a hot heavy based pan, and cook fish quickly, leaving it still glassy and pink inside.

whisk vinegar, salt, pepper, mustard and olive oil.

combine potatoes, beans, tomatoes, cucumber, capsicum, spring onions, anchovy fillets, eggs and olives.

arrange salad on each plate.

break fish into chunks, and tuck into each salad. Pour dressing over top.

SERVES SIX

sicilian stuffed sardines

Any Mediterranean island worth its sea salt knows a thing or two about sardines. Sicily knows more than a thing or two.

1 kilo (2 pounds) fresh sardines

2 tablespoons olive oil

6 tablespoons breadcrumbs

½ cup sultanas

½ cup pine nuts

6 anchovies

½ cup parsley, chopped

1 onion, finely chopped

Freshly ground pepper

1 lemon, quartered

clean, rinse and gut sardines (see page 57), and pat dry.

heat 1 tablespoon oil, add breadcrumbs, and fry until golden.

add breadcrumbs to sultanas, pine nuts, anchovies, parsley, onion, and pepper, and mix well.

stuff each sardine with mixture, close firmly, and pack in one layer on a well-oiled baking dish.

scatter any remaining mixture over the top, sprinkle with remaining olive oil and bake at 200°C (400°F) for 30 minutes until sardines are cooked and topping is golden.

serve with wedges of lemon.

SERVES SIX

spaghetti **with natural tomato sauce**

The shock of the cold, raw tomato against the heat of the pasta brings this dish alive.

6 firm, ripe tomatoes

2 tablespoons extra virgin olive oil

Salt and freshly ground pepper

Fresh green or purple basil leaves

100 grams (4 ounces) spaghetti per person

dunk each tomato in boiling water for a few seconds, remove, and peel skin.

cut each tomato in half, squeeze to discard seeds, and chop the remaining flesh into small dice.

mix tomato with olive oil, salt and pepper to taste, and a few torn basil leaves, and leave to marinate for an hour or so in the refrigerator.

cook the pasta in plenty of boiling, salted water until tender but firm to the bite.

drain and distribute between serving plates.

top with the cold tomato sauce and a few more torn basil leaves, and serve immediately.

SERVES FOUR TO SIX

whiting **in a polenta crust**

A quick pan fry of delicate fish with a crisp cornmeal coating that seals the fish without the need for a thick batter.

8 small whiting fillets

1 cup polenta (ground maize or cornmeal)

2 tablespoons olive oil

1 tablespoon butter

cut 4 tiny slits in the skin of each fillet to stop it from curling when cooked.

press each fillet gently into a plate of polenta.

heat olive oil with butter in a large frypan, and fry fish briskly on both sides.

remove as soon as fish turns white, within 2 or 3 minutes.

serve with spinach with raisins and pine nuts (see page 94), just to give yourself something to do.

SERVES FOUR

spaghetti with natural tomato sauce

grilled *mussels with cumin*

A quick and easy summer lunch if your fishmonger sells cleaned, fresh mussels on the half shell. If not, prepare as shown on page 71.

1 garlic clove, crushed

1 tablespoon parsley, finely chopped

1 tablespoon coriander, finely chopped

Pinch of ground cumin

2 tablespoons soft butter

2 tablespoons breadcrumbs

Freshly ground pepper

24 small fresh raw mussels, on the half shell

heat grill.

beat garlic, herbs, cumin and butter together with a wooden spoon.

add breadcrumbs and pepper.

dab a teaspoonful of the mixture onto each mussel, and grill for 2 minutes until golden and bubbling.

SERVES FOUR

lamburger *with sweet roasted onions*

An easy and impressive summer lunch of pink-grilled lamb served between 'plates' of olive bread (see New Basics, page 216). Serve with a fresh green salad and chilled wine.

20 small onions, peeled

1 tablespoon olive oil

1 tablespoon brown sugar

4 lean lamb fillets

1 cup fetta cheese

1 tablespoon olive oil

Fresh mint leaves

Olive and rosemary bread (see page 216)

 or focaccia

cook onions in simmering, salted water for 5 minutes, then drain.

heat oil in a small frypan, add onions and sugar, and toss to coat.

cook, tossing occasionally, until onions are tender and golden brown.

heat grill or barbecue, and grill lamb fillets quickly until seared on outside, and still pink inside.

rest for 5 minutes.

slice lamb and lay on bread or focaccia.

crumble fetta on top, tuck in roasted onions, drizzle with olive oil and scatter with mint leaves.

top with remaining rounds of olive bread.

SERVES FOUR TO SIX

grilled mussels
with cumin

sardines

Sardines are way too good for your cat. Give moggy a nice porterhouse steak instead, and save the sardines for yourself. Rich in omega 3 fatty acids and full of sea-fresh flavour, they lend themselves to quick and easy cooking.

Scientists now believe that omega 3 fatty acids hold huge potential in the fight against coronary heart disease and inflammatory diseases like rheumatoid arthritis. As well, natural fish oils may help protect the body from high blood pressure, kidney disease, asthma, diabetes and breast cancer.

Even canned sardines are good for you, because they are processed, like canned tuna and salmon, with their own soft, edible calcium-rich bones. They are also rich in iron, a mineral often lacking in womens' diets.

After all that, you can't let a few tiny eyes put you off a healthy meal.

A couple of dollars will get you enough for a meal. Get them home, wash them, and slit the stomachs with a sharp knife.

Clean and rinse the cavity under cold running water, then remove the backbone (if you want to), by snipping it at either end with scissors and pulling it from the tail end with your fingers.

It's entirely up to you as to whether you leave the head on or not.

10 ideas to get you started

layer cleaned sardines in a lightly oiled baking dish, scatter a mixture of minced parsley, garlic, grated parmigiano cheese and breadcrumbs on top, and bake at 200°C (400°F) for 20 minutes.

stuff the same fresh, fragrant breadcrumbs inside each sardine before baking.

roll each one in polenta (cornmeal) before frying for an unusual, crunchy texture.

spread sardines lightly with fine Dijon mustard, sprinkle with breadcrumbs, and grill until golden brown.

flatten them out and marinate for several hours in red wine vinegar, garlic, oregano, salt and pepper, before dredging in flour and deep frying.

dust with a powder of ground cumin, paprika, and salt, and fry in a little olive oil.

stuff each sardine with a spoonful of leftover lemon risotto, and bake.

mix parsley, garlic, grated parmigiano and two beaten eggs, then dip sardines in then before deep frying.

stuff each sardine with a spoonful of leftover mashed potato mixed with chopped parsley, coriander, cumin and paprika, then dip in flour and fry.

just brush with extra virgin olive oil, grill, and serve with wedges of lemon and fresh mint.

new **SALADS**

There are salads, *and there are salads.*

There are the refrigerator refugees of iceberg lettuce, processed cheese and canned vegetables from the past. Then there are museum classics, like the sublime Niçoise.

And there are those of the **here and now**, sparkling plates of snapping fresh seafood drizzled with virgin olive oil, of glossy green spinach spiked with fetta cheese and oregano, of tender chicken tossed in fragrant lime juice and chilli, and of fresh fruit salad in sweet ginger syrup. These are salads that become the **main event**, not something to be tossed to one side.

If your salads are of the common or garden variety, consider turning over a new leaf. These days, the range of mixed greens and cresses at good greengrocers is positively inspirational. There is the delicate lamb's tongue known as mâche; the loose-hearted butter lettuce; the **delicate mignonette** with its permanently pressed frill of green, red or brown leaves; baby spinach; and the crisp and crunchy cos, or romaine lettuce, without which the noble Caesar salad is betrayed. (*Et tu, iceberg?*)

Or go for bold flavours, with feathery leafed mitzuma; cute and curly endive; burgundy coloured oakleaf; **peppery watercress**; and this decade's gastronomic symbol, the feather edged, piquant rocket (arugula) with its distinctive sour, nutty twang.

Salads, like people, should be clean and **well dressed**. Wash the leaves, wrap them in a clean, tea towel and **swing** them with the full length of your arm (do this outside, as the water simply streams out!). Without such tumble drying, your dressiest olive oil and vinegar will slip and slide to the bottom of the bowl instead of coating each leaf.

Then toss some sea salt and a twist of ground pepper into a large bowl. **Splash in the vinegar** (fruity balsamic, sweet raspberry, delicate sherry, hearty red wine), whisk in your chosen oil (extra virgin olive, light grapeseed, seductive walnut), and play with the balance until you like the taste. That's it.

You can go on, adding spoonfuls of serendipity in the form of Dijon mustard, white wine, basil pesto, capers, lemon zest, walnuts, caraway seeds, lightly crushed garden herbs, or shavings of nutty parmigiano. Just remember it's a **salad**, not a smorgasbord.

green beans
with sesame
RECIPE 62
——
the I'd-
forgotten-it-
was-so-good
caesar salad
RECIPE 62
——

green **beans with sesame**

A refreshingly sweet vinaigrette gives fresh green beans an Asian accent. You'll find sesame oil and mirin at any Asian food store.

300 grams (11 ounces) green beans

2 teaspoons sesame oil

2 teaspoons mirin

1 teaspoon white sesame seeds

cut the top stem from each bean.

cook beans in simmering, salted water until just tender.

mix sesame oil, mirin and sesame seeds.

drain beans and toss them in the dressing immediately.

serve cold.

SERVES TWO TO FOUR

the **I'd-forgotten-it-was-so-good caesar salad**

Crisp lettuce lashed with parmigiano, crunchy croutons and anchovies and lightly coated in a lemony, creamy dressing.

2 cos (romaine) lettuces

4 slices of stale white bread or focaccia

1 garlic clove

1 teaspoon olive oil

1 teaspoon dried oregano

1 teaspoon grated lemon rind

1 free range egg

1 to 2 tablespoons lemon juice

Salt and freshly ground pepper

1 teaspoon white wine vinegar

½ cup good olive oil

10 anchovies, rinsed and dried

1 tablespoon freshly grated parmigiano

Shavings of parmigiano

wash and dry lettuce leaves.

rub bread with cut garlic clove, brush with olive oil, sprinkle with oregano and bake at 160°C (325°F) until crisp.

combine lemon rind, egg, juice, salt, pepper and vinegar in a small bowl and whisk.

add olive oil slowly, whisking constantly until smooth, and coat leaves in dressing.

add anchovies and parmigiano, and arrange in salad bowl.

tuck croutons and cheese shavings (best done with potato peeler) into leaves and serve immediately.

SERVES FOUR

grilled **potato salad**

Caraway seeds add nuttiness to slices of spicy grilled potato. Serve with homemade mayonnaise spiced up with ground cumin (see New Basics, page 215).

6 red-skinned potatoes (pontiac or desirée)

2 tablespoons fine vinegar

3 tablespoons virgin olive oil

1 teaspoon ground turmeric

1 teaspoon dried oregano

Salt and freshly ground pepper

1 tablespoon caraway seeds

cook potatoes in simmering, salted water until almost tender.

drain and cool.

mix vinegar, olive oil, turmeric, oregano, pepper and salt.

cut potatoes into 1 cm (½ in) slices, and brush with mixture.

leave for 1 hour to absorb flavours.

sprinkle each slice with a few caraway seeds and grill until crisp, turning once.

SERVES SIX

grilled potato
salad

saigon **salad rolls**

Fresh prawns, noodles, lettuce and mint, tied together with chives or spring onions, make a very glam 'Nam appetiser.

200 grams (7 ounces) rice vermicelli

4 chives or spring onion greens

1 iceberg lettuce

12 small prawns, cooked and peeled

Fresh mint leaves

Nuoc cham sauce (see New Basics, page 214)

toss vermicelli into a big pot of boiling water for 5 minutes, or until tender.

dunk chives or spring onion greens into boiling water, to soften.

rinse noodles and chives in cold water, and drain.

cut a length of noodles, wrap in lettuce leaf, and tie together with chive, tucking in 3 prawns and some mint leaves as you go.

serve with nuoc cham sauce for dipping.

MAKES FOUR

slow-roasted **tomato and white bean salad**

A satisfying salad of well-seasoned beans topped with the sweet acidic sparkle of roasted tomatoes.

300 grams (11 ounces) white cannellini beans

6 cloves

1 onion, peeled

6 whole vine-ripened tomatoes

2 garlic cloves, lightly smashed

1 cup fresh mint leaves, torn

2 tablespoons extra virgin olive oil

1 tablespoon wine vinegar

soak beans overnight, and drain.

stick cloves in onion, and add to pot with beans and cold water to cover.

bring to the boil, and simmer for 30 to 40 minutes until cooked.

strain and set aside.

dunk tomatoes in boiling water for a few seconds, and peel.

place tomatoes and garlic in a roasting pan and drizzle with a little olive oil.

bake at 160°C (325°F) for 1 hour, until tomatoes soften and start to lose shape.

mix olive oil and vinegar, and season.

toss beans and mint in dressing, and spoon onto each plate.

top with a still warm tomato and serve.

SERVES SIX

yoghurt cheese and quail egg salad

Do-it-yourself cheese made from natural yoghurt is teamed with little hard-boiled quail eggs and served with crusty bread.

1 dozen quail eggs, from a chicken specialist

12 yoghurt cheese balls (see New Basics,
    page 217)

Mixed baby greens (rocket, curly endive,
    oakleaf)

2 tablespoons walnut or olive oil

1 tablespoon white wine vinegar

Salt and freshly ground pepper

place quail eggs into a pot of cold water, bring to boil, and boil for 2 minutes.

drain, and cool eggs in cold running water.

peel eggs and cut in half.

scatter washed and dried lettuce leaves on a large flat plate.

arrange eggs and cheese among leaves.

mix vinegar, salt and pepper, slowly whisk in oil, and drizzle over leaves.

SERVES SIX

cucumber and chilli salad

Little lettuce cups hold a tangy, fresh, crisp and crunchy salad. Serve with a Thai hot and sour soup, seafood salad, or at your very un-Thai barbecue.

1 continental cucumber

1 purple onion, finely sliced

1 teaspoon sugar

2 tablespoons lime juice

2 tablespoons fish sauce (nam pla)

2 fresh red chillies, sliced

1 iceberg lettuce

2 tablespoons beer nuts

slice cucumber in half lengthways, remove seeds with spoon, and finely slice.

mix cucumber with onion.

dissolve sugar in lime juice, add fish sauce and chillies, and toss through cucumber and onion.

peel leaves from lettuce to form 4 cups.

spoon salad into lettuce cups and top with nuts.

SERVES FOUR

white **bean tonnato**

You may have heard of vitello tonnato, a strange but wonderful dish of cold veal in a creamy tuna sauce. Well, this is white bean tonnato. I made it up.

250 grams (9 ounces) dried white cannellini
   beans

1 tablespoon olive oil

1 tablespoon fresh mint, torn

1 tablespoon parsley, chopped

350 gram (12 ounce) can of tuna in olive oil

4 anchovies

2 tablespoons small capers

Juice of 1 lemon, at least

½ cup virgin olive oil

½ cup natural yoghurt

1 extra tablespoon small capers

soak beans in cold water overnight, drain and place in pot of cold water.

cook for 30 to 40 minutes until tender.

drain, toss in olive oil and herbs, and arrange in serving dish.

combine tuna, anchovies, capers and lemon juice in a blender and process to a fine paste.

add oil while motor is running.

taste for seasoning, and stir in yoghurt.

spoon tuna sauce over beans, and scatter extra capers on top.

chill for 2 or 3 hours before serving to allow flavours to mingle.

SERVES FOUR

thai **chicken and mint salad**

A refreshing, tangy salad of sliced chicken and herbs that makes a zingy beginning to any meal.

2 chicken breasts

2 lemon grass stalks, tender white part only

2 tablespoons spring onion, finely chopped

2 tablespoons shallots, finely sliced

2 tablespoons fresh mint, finely chopped

2 tablespoons fresh coriander, finely chopped

2 tablespoons fish sauce (nam pla)

2 tablespoons lime juice

1 teaspoon sugar

2 red chillies, sliced

remove skin from chicken, and grill until just cooked.

slice into very thin slices.

cut lemon grass into very fine slices.

mix lemon grass with chicken, spring onions, shallots, mint and coriander.

combine fish sauce, lime juice, sugar and chillies until sugar dissolves, then toss through salad.

SERVES FOUR

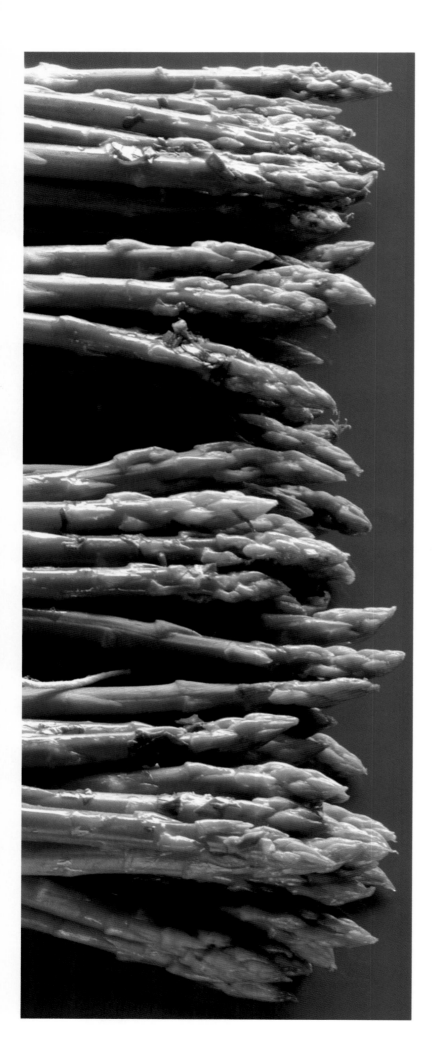

asparagus **with lemon and coriander**

Celebrate fresh asparagus season by serving it simply dressed with a lemony vinaigrette of Asian oils and fresh coriander.

1 kilo (2 pounds) fresh asparagus

1 tablespoon lemon juice

1 tablespoon coriander, finely chopped

1 tablespoon peanut oil

1 teaspoon sesame oil

1 teaspoon soy sauce

Freshly ground pepper

wash and trim asparagus, tie into even bundles with kitchen string, and lower into gently simmering salted water.

cook for a few minutes, to retain a crunch.

drain and refresh under cold running water to 'set' the colour.

whisk dressing ingredients together, pour over asparagus and serve.

SERVES SIX

asparagus with
lemon and
coriander

warm **potato and mussel salad**

A frothy saffron sauce coats this lovely salad of warm potatoes and mussels. Put out plenty of crusty bread to mop up the sauce.

2 kilo (4 pounds) mussels

1 kilo (2 pounds) red-skinned potatoes

Juice of 1 lemon

2 tablespoons extra virgin olive oil

Freshly ground pepper

Pinch of genuine saffron powder

1 tablespoon butter, cut into cubes

1 tablespoon chervil or parsley, finely chopped

cook mussels according to method shown on page 71.

strain juices through a fine strainer or wet muslin cloth, and reserve.

cook potatoes in boiling, salted water until cooked but still firm.

drain, and slice into 1 cm (½ in) slices.

coat potato in olive oil, lemon juice and pepper, and arrange with mussels on serving plates.

heat reserved mussel juices and saffron in a small pan, and whisk in butter until sauce is frothy.

pour over salad and scatter with herbs.

SERVES SIX

world's **greatest salad dressing**

A creamy, light salad dressing recipe that will hold you in good stead all year round. Pour it over asparagus, spinach, beetroot, salads, cold meats, and almost anything you can think of.

2 free range eggs

½ cup red wine vinegar

1 tablespoon Dijon mustard

1 teaspoon paprika

Salt

1 teaspoon sugar

1 cup grapeseed oil

place eggs, vinegar, mustard, paprika, salt and sugar in food processor, and blend.

continue to blend while slowly pouring grapeseed oil into mixture.

that's it.

warm potato
and mussel
salad

Let's face it, shellfish are scary. There are beady-eyed monsters in shell-like suits of armour, mighty warrior crabs with snap-your-arm-off pincers, prickly sea urchins, and slammed-shut clams. Spielberg's monsters are pussycats compared to what's sitting on your kitchen bench ready to be turned into tonight's dinner.

Nothing is as exciting, as delicious, and as addictive as very, very fresh shellfish. If you aren't excited by the sweetness of your lobster, the bouncy freshness of your prawns, the delicacy of your scallops, the deep-sea flavour of your crabs, and the sea-salty brininess of your freshly-opened oysters, then they're simply not fresh.

There is only one way to ensure total freshness, and that is to take a deep breath and buy your shellfish alive. If not alive, then green (raw).

When you've done it once or twice, you'll be hooked on the flavour. You'll get to know your fishmonger intimately, arm yourself with rubber gloves, designer pliers, and long-handled tongs, and you'll never walk sideways when you see a crab again.

Southern rock lobster (crayfish)

There is no easy way to kill a lobster. The best way, for you and for it, seems to be to drown it in a big pot of covered cold water for at least an hour, under a weighted lid.

Then cook it in simmering, salted water for 5 minutes for the first 450 grams (pound), and 3 minutes thereafter for each 450 grams (pound).

Or place it in a hot pan, drizzle with olive oil and roast in a hot oven until the shell turns red, which will take around 15 minutes for a 1 kilo (2 pound) size.

Oysters

When it comes to opening oysters, you are as good as your tools. Invest in a good, strong oyster knife, wrap a tea towel around your hand to protect it from any slips, insert the tip of the knife into the hinged end of the oyster, and wriggle it across to find the connecting muscle. Twist the blade of the knife to open the shell. Try not to lose the juices as you do this.

If eating them raw, leave the juices in each shell. If cooking, strain juices through 2 thicknesses of damp muslin, and use the juices in your cooking.

Prawns

Buy green (raw) prawns, toss them into a big pot of boiling, salted water, and remove them as they rise to the surface.

Or cook them in a hot pan, lightly slicked with oil, for just a few minutes until still glassy in the centre.

You can devein the prawn before cooking by hooking a slender wooden satay stick gently through the back of the 'neck'. Lightly lever the skewer away from the prawn, and it will bring the black intestinal tract with it.

Pipis and clams

Soak, prepare and cook as for mussels, removing them as soon as they open.

Scallops

Scallops are best bought on the shell, and need very little cooking. Slip the blade of a short, sharp knife between the shells and twist the knife to open shell. Twist the top shell away from the lower one, and slice under the flesh to detach it from its shell. Detach dark intestine.

If buying shelled scallops, specify 'dry' rather than 'washed'. Washed scallops are more water than scallop.

Shovel-nosed lobster (Moreton Bay or Balmain bugs)

Use a heavy Chinese cleaver to simply cleave the bug in 2 lengthwise. Pull out the black intestinal tract and the raw meat. Otherwise, cook whole in plenty of boiling, salted water for around 3 minutes.

Crab

As a general rule, drown the crab in fresh water for a couple of hours, under a weighted lid. Cook in plenty of boiling, salted water (around 8 minutes for blue swimmer crabs and 10 minutes for spanner crabs). Boil mud crabs and king crabs until the shell turns bright red, around 8 minutes per 500 grams (pound).

Use a knife to lever the shell off from the rear, and clean fronds and spongy bits away.

Split each crab into quarters, and crack legs to get at the meat.

Mussels

Soak mussels in cold water for 2 or 3 hours, changing water 3 times. Throw out any with broken shells, any which float, or any which do not close. Scrub clean under cold running water and yank the little beards from the shells.

Heat 2 tablespoons olive oil in a pan, and fry 2 garlic cloves until they colour.

Add 1 cup of white wine, 6 black peppercorns, 4 parsley stalks and 1 kilo (2 pounds) mussels, cover and turn up the heat.

Shake the pan with all your might after a minute or two of cooking, and remove any mussels that have opened.

Cover and return to the heat for another minute, then shake and check for more opened mussels. Repeat process, discarding any mussels that don't open at all.

Drain the cooking juices through a fine strainer or muslin cloth, and reserve.

Yabbies

A close enough cousin to France's écrevisse to make the French madly jealous, yabbies are as common as mud in the country farm dams of Australia. Cook in boiling, salted water for a minute or two until the shells turn bright red.

Cool, then twist the tail away from the head, and use your thumb to 'peel' the underside of the tail away to reveal the flesh.

F I S H

new SOUPS

black-eyed bean
and sausage
soup
RECIPE 79

Soup can save people's lives.

Soup nourishes and nurtures us, giving us strength to be **decent, human folk** in an indecent, inhuman world. Soup brings us to our senses. It has the power and the **beauty** to make the heart glad, the pulse quicken, and the tastebuds tingle. Soup is hot. Cold soup is a contradiction in terms, like hot ice-cream.

Soup is the **hot water bottle** of the food world. It goes swimmingly with winter nights, board games, glasses of wine, toasted croutons, and oven-warm bread. It is more satisfying than fluffy slippers, more nutritious than hot chocolate, and more ideologically sound than a fur coat.

Soup is what you have when it's too late to have lunch and too early to have tea, or when it's too late to have dinner and too early to go to bed. There is something **subversive** and mischievous about soup, like staying out late, or skipping school.

Above all, soup is all about true, hearty flavour that cannot be cheated. Whether your base stock comes from vegetables, fish or chicken (see New Basics, pages 212–13), it must be **good and honest**. Use the fast vegetable soup recipe to clear the kitchen of any vegetables lying around at the end of the weekend, and you'll have a beautiful soup to sustain you during the week.

The nicest thing about soup is that it cannot be pretentious. Elaborate pastry domes, fiddly lace biscuits and creatively drizzled cream are best left in the gastronomic museums of the past. Soup is **elbows on the table**, good wine in the glasses, and a little snack on the side, such as grilled bread slicked with garlic oil, fritters of spring onion and parsley, or freshly made cheesy scones.

For a spicy Malaysian curry laksa, or subtle Cantonese rice congee, add a few baby spring rolls, prawn dumplings, or steamed roast pork buns.

Soup is a reminder, after the table-hopping of the last decade or so, of good food, **good friends** and good times. It doesn't try to buy your pleasure, it just helps you relax and enjoy yourself. So just go with the flow.

french bistro
onion soup
RECIPE 78

fast vegetable soup

A magical soup to make when you desperately feel like something fresh and easy but don't quite know what.

1 tablespoon butter

1 onion, finely sliced

2 leeks, cleaned and sliced

½ cabbage, shredded

2 potatoes, peeled

2 carrots, peeled

Celery, lettuce leaves, turnips, pumpkin, beans, zucchini, parsley, or anything else found lying around in the refrigerator

1.5 litres (1½ quarts) boiling water

Salt and freshly ground pepper

A little nutmeg, grated

1 tablespoon butter to finish

Freshly grated parmigiano

melt butter in frypan, and gently cook onion and leeks until soft.

cut or shred all other vegetables, and cook, stirring often, until they start to soften.

add boiling water, salt and pepper, and cook over low heat for 30 minutes.

stir in a little grated nutmeg and the final tablespoon of butter and serve with a bowl of parmigiano.

SERVES SIX

beautiful beetroot borscht

This is worth doing for the divinely deep colour alone, although the flavour makes it one of the great soups of the world.

6 beetroot

2 potatoes

2 carrots

1 bay leaf

Few sprigs of fresh thyme

2 cups chicken stock

1 teaspoon plain white vinegar

Fresh dill

Sour cream

scrub beetroot and cook in simmering, salted water until tender, for about an hour.

peel off skin under cold running water.

cut beetroot into cubes and reserve.

strain beetroot stock through a fine sieve and reserve.

peel potatoes and carrots and cut into cubes the same size as the beetroot.

cook potatoes, carrots, thyme and bay leaf in chicken stock at a gentle simmer for 15 minutes or until tender.

add cubed beetroot and beetroot stock to make up desired quantity, and heat.

add vinegar, and serve.

top with dill and serve with sour cream.

SERVES FOUR

fragrant chicken soup with rice noodles

A soupy meal that's a daily favourite in Vietnam, where it is known as pho, (pronounced 'fah'). Lime juice, chilli and fish sauce blast it — and you — out of the comfort zone.

1 medium free range chicken, cleaned

3 litres (4 quarts) water

Salt

5 cm (2 in) knob of fresh ginger, peeled

2 onions, peeled and thinly sliced

2 tablespoons fish sauce

6 peppercorns

400 grams (14 ounces) fresh rice noodles

2 spring onions, finely sliced

1 lime or lemon, quartered

2 fresh red chillies, sliced

Bunch of Asian basil or mint

Bunch of fresh coriander

Fresh bean sprouts, washed and trimmed

place chicken, water, salt, ginger and onions in a large pot and bring to the boil.
skim off any froth, lower the heat and cook gently for 45 minutes.
remove chicken, remove breasts and legs from chicken and return carcass to the pot.
add fish sauce and peppercorns, and cook gently for 2 hours, skimming occasionally.
strain stock through a fine sieve.
remove cooked meat from chicken breast and legs, and slice finely.
cut noodles into tagliatelle-like strips.
pour boiling water over noodles and separate the strands.

divide noodles between 4 deep soup bowls, add sliced chicken, and top with soup.
add spring onions.
serve with platters of quartered limes, sliced chillies, lots of Asian basil, coriander and bean sprouts for each person to add according to their taste.

SERVES FOUR

french bistro onion soup

Au Pied de Cochon is a busy, bright, bedazzling bistro open 24 hours a day in Les Halles, Paris. Their famous onion soup is rich and sweet, with a crusty, toasted top.

450 grams (1 pound) white onions, thinly sliced

2 cups dry white wine

1 tablespoon unsalted butter

1 litre (1 quart) chicken stock

6 slices of crusty, thin breadstick

½ cup good freshly grated gruyère

cook onions, wine and butter in a heavy bottomed pan over low heat, uncovered, for about 40 minutes, until onion is soft and most of the liquid is absorbed.
distribute the onions among 6 warmed bowls, and top with simmering stock.
place a round of bread on top of each soup, top bread with grated cheese.
grill for 2 or 3 minutes until the cheese melts into a glorious, golden brown mess.
serve immediately.

SERVES SIX

chicken **dumpling soup**

Fresh leaves of parsley mingle with delicious little balls of fragrant chicken in sparkling clear chicken stock. A great late-night supper soup.

250 grams (9 ounces) minced chicken

1 tablespoon chopped parsley

1 tablespoon chopped basil

1 tablespoon grated parmigiano

2 tablespoons fine dry breadcrumbs

1 tablespoon soft butter

1 free range egg

Pinch of nutmeg

1 litre (1 quart) good chicken stock

Salt and freshly ground black pepper

Fresh flat-leaf parsley

whizz everything except chicken stock into a fine paste in the blender.

roll small spoonfuls of mixture into balls until you have around 20.

drop chicken dumplings into simmering chicken stock for 5 minutes or until cooked.

scoop out dumplings, and distribute among warmed bowls.

taste soup for salt and pepper, and quickly strain into the bowls.

add a few extra leaves of flat-leaf parsley and serve hot.

SERVES FOUR

black-eyed **bean and sausage soup**

A hale and hearty soup sweetened with pumpkin and beefed up with beans and tiny chipolata sausages from a good deli or European butcher.

450 grams (1 pound) pumpkin

2 onions

2 garlic cloves, unpeeled

1 tablespoon olive oil

1 cup black-eyed beans, soaked overnight

1 carrot, peeled and chopped

350 gram (12 ounce) can of tomatoes

10 cups chicken stock or water

6 chipolata sausages

Salt and freshly ground pepper

2 tablespoons chopped parsley

chop pumpkin and onion into rough wedges, toss with garlic and oil in roasting pan and bake at 180°C (360°F) for 1 hour.

cut off skins, and chop flesh.

drain beans, place in large pot with carrots and plenty of cold water, and cook for 30 minutes.

combine pumpkin, onion, garlic, tomatoes, beans, carrots, salt and pepper and add stock or boiling water.

cook for another 20 minutes, stirring occasionally.

prick sausages and grill until well-browned. Add to soup with parsley, and serve with crusty bread.

SERVES SIX

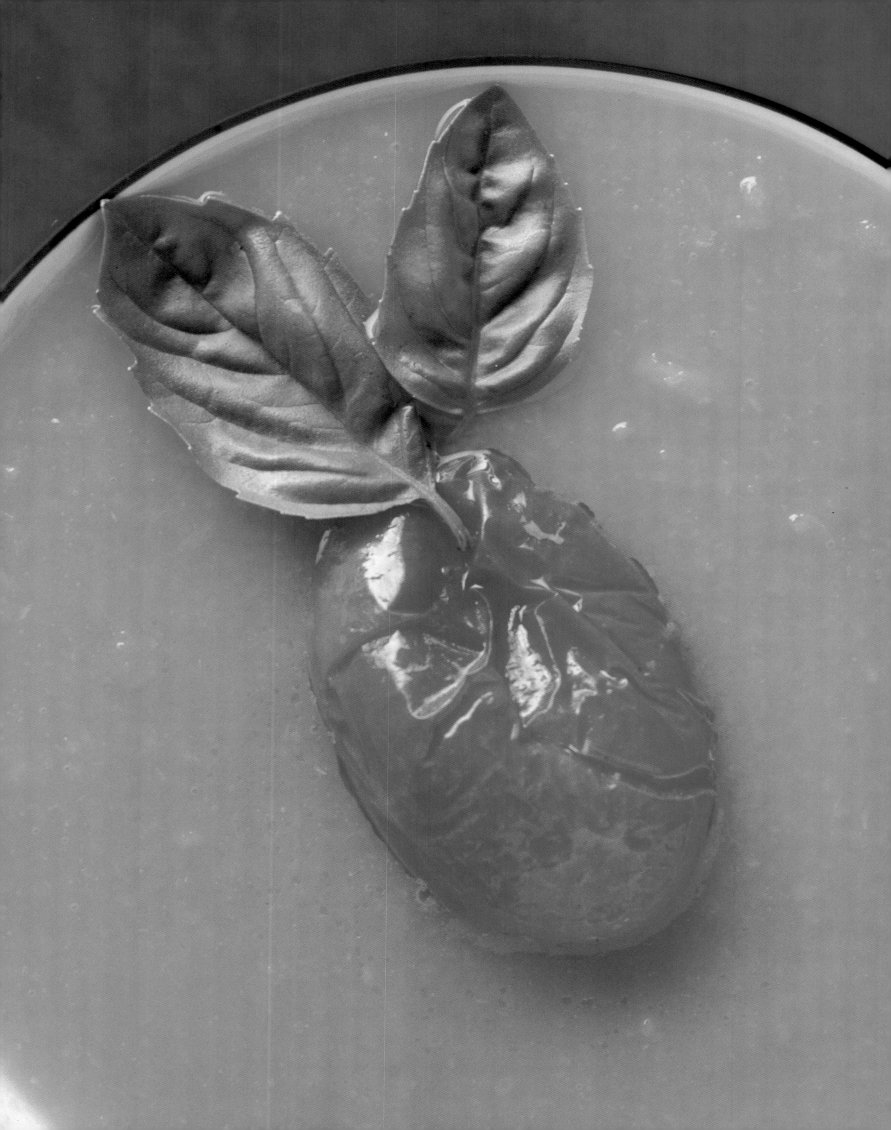

carrot **and cumin soup with slow-roasted tomatoes**

Like many good vegetable soups, you can make this with stock or with water. Serve with a slow-roasted tomato (see New Basics, page 211) for a surprise burst of flavour.

1 kilo (2 pounds) carrots

2 medium onions, peeled

1 tablespoon olive oil

1 tablespoon butter

½ teaspoon saffron powder or a few saffron
  threads

1 garlic clove

1 cup dry white wine

1 litre (1 quart) water

Pinch of cayenne pepper

Pinch of ground cumin

Salt

scrub carrots and cut into large chunks.

peel onions and chop.

heat oil and butter, add onions, saffron and garlic and cook for 20 minutes.

add wine and bring to the boil.

add carrots and water or stock, and simmer until carrots are cooked.

whizz soup in food processor, gently reheat, add cayenne and cumin, taste for salt, and serve.

SERVES FOUR TO SIX

roasted **red pepper soup**

The smoky, sweet flavour of roasted red capsicums is brilliant in any form, but particularly in a vibrant, colourful soup.

10 red capsicums

350 gram (12 ounce) can of plum tomatoes

1 litre (1 quart) chicken stock

Good pinch of salt

Good pinch of cayenne pepper

roast capsicums on baking tray in 200°C (400°F) oven for around 30 minutes, until skin bubbles and darkens.

leave in a covered bowl for 10 minutes, then peel, keeping any juices and discarding skin and seeds.

place flesh, juice, and tomatoes in food processor and blend.

pour mixture through a sieve, pushing against the mesh to extract maximum colour and flavour.

heat with chicken stock, add salt and cayenne pepper, and serve hot.

SERVES FOUR

fish soup with saffron and potatoes

A deliciously rich and healthy golden bowl of potatoes, zucchini, deep sea fish and prawns flavoured with saffron and fresh herbs.

1 tablespoon olive oil

1 onion, sliced

3 garlic cloves, crushed

350 gram (12 ounce) can of tomatoes

2 tablespoons tomato paste

1 tablespoon fresh basil, torn

1 litre (1 quart) fish stock (see New Basics, page 213)

1 bay leaf

4 potatoes, chopped

6 zucchini, sliced

1/2 teaspoon cayenne pepper

2 strips of orange peel

1/2 teaspoon saffron powder or a few saffron threads

Salt and freshly ground pepper

450 grams (1 pound) fish fillets, roughly chopped or cutlets (schnapper, ling, dory)

8 green prawns, shelled but with tails intact

heat olive oil and cook onion and garlic until onion is soft.

add tomatoes, tomato paste and basil and simmer for 15 minutes.

add fish stock, bay leaf and potatoes and simmer for 30 minutes.

add zucchini, cayenne, peel, saffron, salt and pepper and cook for 10 minutes.

add fillets or whole cutlets and prawns, cover and simmer for 5 minutes.

SERVES FOUR

chinese rice congee

Standard breakfast fare in Guangzhou (Canton), congee is a creamy, pure, bland porridge of rice and chicken stock, to which you can add snappy accessories like slices of raw fish or barbecued roast meats. I love it for lunch on the run, or for a late supper with a glass of champagne.

1 cup short grain rice

10 cups cold water or chicken stock, or half and half

Accompaniments

Smoked fish, pickled vegetables, salted peanuts, sliced fresh ginger, sliced roast pork, sliced cooked chicken, sea scallops, roasted shallots, fish sauce, coriander, or just spring onion greens

rinse rice under cold running water until the water runs clear, not cloudy.

combine rice and stock or water in a large pot, and bring to the boil.

cover pot and simmer very gently for 2 hours or more, stirring occasionally, until rice dissolves into a thick and creamy soup.

add more water if too thick, or cook longer if too thin.

heretics can add salt and pepper at this point, but the flavour is meant to be pure.

serve in small bowls with platters of accompaniments to add to the soup.

SERVES FOUR

curry **laksa**

This is one of the world's great deep and meaningful soup and noodle meals, with just the right balance of tang, spice and creamy coconut milk.

Paste

2 lemon grass stalks, white part only

2 garlic cloves

2.5 cm (1 in) piece fresh ginger

5 candlenuts or macadamia nuts

1 teaspoon blachan (shrimp paste)

3 dried chillies, soaked

1 teaspoon turmeric powder

½ teaspoon coriander powder

1 onion, peeled and chopped

1 teaspoon ground cumin

Soup

8 fresh green (raw) prawns

3 tablespoons vegetable oil

2 cups water

2 cups chicken stock

2 cups coconut milk

2 kaffir lime leaves or grated rind of 1 lime

6 fried beancurd cakes

1 teaspoon sugar

Salt

250 grams (9 ounces) rice vermicelli (rice stick noodles)

250 grams (9 ounces) thick yellow wheat noodles (hokkien)

1 cup bean shoots

1 tablespoon fresh coriander leaves

1 tablespoon mint leaves

4 spring onions, finely chopped

grind all paste ingredients together.

shell and devein prawns and set aside.

fry prawn shells and heads in a little of the oil until fragrant, add water and stock, simmer for 10 minutes, then strain.

heat remaining oil in a large frypan and fry the paste until fragrant.

add stock and bring to the boil.

reduce heat and add coconut milk, stirring constantly.

add prawns, kaffir lime leaves, sliced beancurd cakes, sugar and salt, and simmer for 5 minutes until prawns are cooked.

cook the rice vermicelli in boiling water for 5 minutes.

pour boiling water over the hokkien noodles and bean shoots and leave until the noodles soften, then drain and rinse under cold water.

place all noodles and bean shoots in each deep serving bowl and ladle soup on top.

top with coriander, mint and spring onions.

SERVES FOUR

It's early on Sunday morning, but already the sunshine is as warm as a breakfast croissant. Pad down to the kitchen and indulge in a precious summer ritual. Grab three or four ripe summer tomatoes, slice them, salt them and douse them in the purest, most innocent extra virgin olive oil you can buy. Toss in a couple of basil leaves and a slightly smashed garlic and leave to marinate, while you crawl back into bed, do your stretching exercises, or read the papers. There is no guarantee that this pleasant summer ritual will tone your body or improve your mind, but it will certainly enhance your weekend. From now on, you are socially secure.

If friends drop in, all you have to do is drizzle a little of this magical, basil-infused oil onto slices of crusty country bread, grill, and top with the reserved tomatoes and basil for a stunning, sun-drenched bruschetta.

Or toss some cooked linguini with the tomatoes, olive oil and basil for a mind-blowing summer lunch or supper.

Or pile the tomatoes into a focaccia sandwich with slices of fresh bocconcini, prosciutto and mint.

Add small black olives and anchovies, and arrange the lot on a pizza base.

Tumble the tomatoes and basil with cooked lobster or prawns.

Serve them as a side salad, with crisped thin slices of deep-fried eggplant and chargrilled lamb fillet.

Layer them with thin slices of purple-skinned onions, top with breadcrumbs, dot with butter and bake au gratin.

Build a pyramid with the tomatoes, layered with slices of fresh bocconcini and plenty of basil leaves, and drizzle the lot with balsamic vinegar.

Or just add things, and keep adding them, to end up with a fabulous summer salad: avocado, ham, oakleaf lettuce, cucumber, artichoke hearts, olives, sun-dried tomatoes, potatoes, spring onions, pine nuts, and capers.

I could go on, but I won't. You should.

The best tomatoes are homegrown ones, because they come with love, care, sunshine, and the irresistible perfume of the tomato plant. Store-bought tomatoes can be improved by keeping them, not in the fridge, but in a closed paper bag for a day or two so that their own naturally produced ethylene gas ripens them.

Don't overlook the Italian plum tomato when cooking. It has less juice, more flesh, and more flavour than the common or garden beefsteak variety. And keep an eye out for sweet Adelaide tomatoes, luscious vine-ripened beauties from Currumbin, and low-acid, sunny yellow tomatoes.

Another month or two and their rich ripeness will be gone, along with the slow sunsets, beach picnics, sundresses, and bare feet. So celebrate the big red before the big chill sets in.

toma

toes

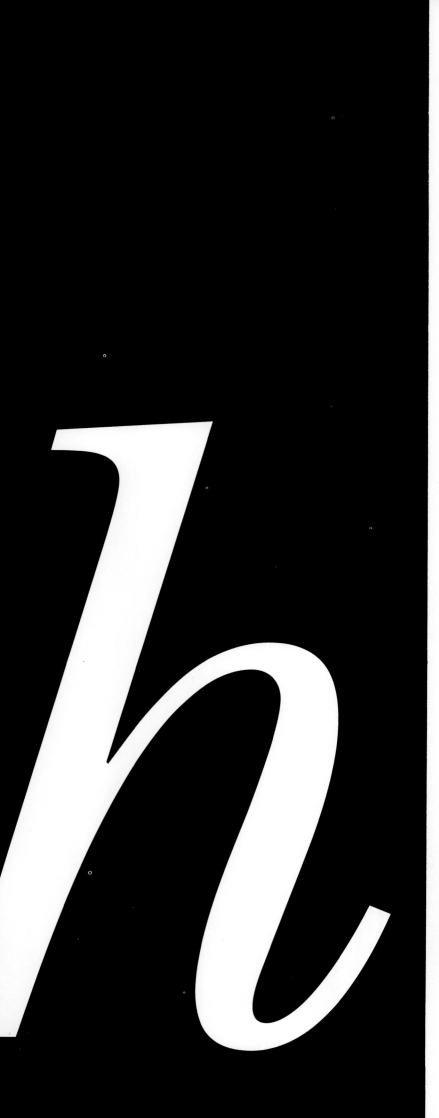

Why in the world are we spending so much time and money on developing additives, flavour boosters and texture enhancers when we can just go and pick some fresh herbs instead?

Herbs contain no artificial colourings or flavourings, no processing and no packaging; just health and happiness and fragrance and flavour.

Basil and tomatoes, oregano and pizza, rosemary and lamb, mint and long summer drinks, chives and potatoes, dill and cucumbers, coriander and curries. Whatever you eat, it will taste better, look better and be better for you with that final flourish of freshness that can only come from herbs.

Asian Mint

A peppery, hot plant with a slender, pointed leaf that spikes up stir fries and makes the hot mint chutney for your next Indian curry.

Basil

Shred the sprightly, peppery basil leaves rather than chop them, and don't eat a tomato without them. When it's plentiful, make pesto (see New Basics, page 210) and you'll never have pallid pasta again.

Chervil

The French chef's favourite, chervil is an elegant, feminine lacy leafed herb that turns omelettes, salads and sauces into French masterpieces in minutes. Fabulous when chopped fresh into a potato salad studded with crisp bacon.

Chives

Lively chives add a delicate onion flavour to scrambled eggs, mayonnaise dressings, leek and potato soup, or baked potatoes topped with sour cream.

Coriander

A musty perfume and a clove-like, pungent flavour make the soft, pretty leaves of coriander a must, whether east meets west or not.

Dill

A delicate herb best used at the last minute as a fashion accessory to salmon, ocean trout, scallops, or on steamed baby vegetables.

Marjoram

A more ladylike cousin of the robust oregano, marjoram is delicious in stuffings, sausages, baked potato dishes, and on buttered vegetables.

Mint

Sweet, refreshing, cooling and minty, mint is a breath of fresh air for lamb, fruit salads, and long summer drinks. A bowl of yoghurt, grated cucumber and mint will take the heat off the hottest curry.

Oregano

A rough-and-tough peasant herb that makes its pungent presence felt on pizza, lamb, Greek moussaka, fetta cheese, and in bolognaise sauce.

Parsley

Not just a frilly garnish in the butcher's window, but an incredibly versatile and popular herb that can go anywhere, anytime. At its best in tabouleh salad, a moist garden mulch of parsley and cracked wheat drenched in lemon juice.

Rosemary

For that irresistible Mediterranean touch, scatter rosemary on your baking bread, into your minestrone soup, and onto roasting meats. Strip the leaves off, and soak the stems in water for an hour before using them as natural skewers for prawns on the grill.

Sage

Stuff duckling with sage and onion, pan fry the narrow, downy leaves with slices of young veal, and chop a little sage into your next apple pie.

Tarragon

Aromatic and spicy tarragon is the classic herb for ye olde bearnaise, hollandaise and tartare sauces, but is equally at home with mushrooms, broad beans, and roast chicken.

Thyme

A pretty little herb that makes the most of grilled fish, or of absolutely anything with olives, capers and anchovies in it. Don't ever eat fresh goat's cheese without it.

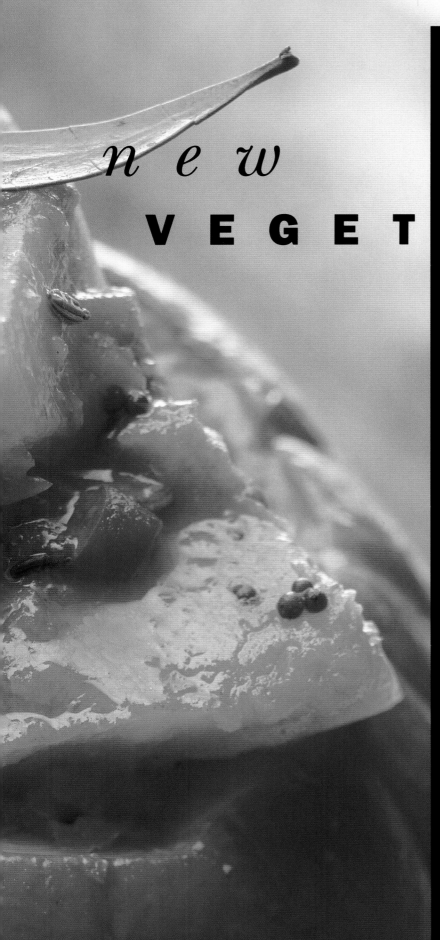

new
VEGETABLES

Vegetables are savagely beautiful things, symbols of a time when our eating was closely linked to our farming. If you have ever picked peas from the plant, dug up some baby carrots, picked **sun-warmed tomatoes** from the vine or run from the garden to the pot with your first harvest of sorrel leaves, you will know what I mean.

Vegetables are not boring.

Everyone who loves good food loves vegetables. With vegetables, you get a massive serving of vibrant colours, startling flavours and **good health**.

We all know why we should eat our vegetables: broccoli, tomatoes, spinach, watercress, green and red capsicums, brussel sprouts, sweet potatoes and kale for vitamins C, E, and beta carotene; and orange vegetables like carrots and pumpkin, or dark, green, leafy vegetables for even more beta carotene. And we know that vegetables also bring us the **anti-oxidants** we need to reduce cholesterol, and to lower the risk of breast and bowel cancer. Even kids know that beans are **nutrition city**.

But do we know how to make vegetables the main event, rather than something tired on the side? Do we think of vegetables when we ask each other what we feel like for dinner? If we trained our brains to **think of vegetables**, grains or pasta as our first choice, and meat or poultry as our second, our bodies would be a lot better off.

To get the maximum vitamin hit from vegetables, buy fresh and eat raw. Get out of the habit of peeling everything. Vegetables like being cooked in **their skins**, in the same way that meat likes to be cooked on the bone. If cooking, leave preparation to the last minute, cook as quickly as possible and eat immediately.

Vegetables go with **good olive oil** and real butter, not margarine and other butter substitutes that are higher in saturated fats. A lot of vegetables like a good squeeze of **lemon juice** or a dash of vinegar at the last minute, to spike up their flavour. Like us, all they want is a little respect, and they are yours for life.

Oh, and make sure you eat them all up, or there won't be any dessert.

potatoes with
thyme and
tomatoes
RECIPE 92

potatoes **with thyme and tomatoes**

A fragrant, delicious dish of layered slices of potato and tomato scented with thyme.

6 medium tomatoes

8 medium potatoes

1 tablespoon butter

2 tablespoons fresh thyme

1 bay leaf, crumbled

Salt and freshly ground pepper

dunk tomatoes in boiling water for 10 seconds, then peel off skin.

cut tomatoes in half, squeeze to remove seeds, slice thinly and set aside.

peel potatoes, and slice thinly.

set oven at 220°C (425°F), and lightly butter a flameproof and ovenproof baking dish with a layer of potatoes.

layer with slices of tomato, thyme, bay leaf, salt and pepper.

cover with a layer of potatoes and repeat, finishing with a final layer of potatoes.

dob any remaining butter on top.

pour boiling water into the dish until it comes halfway up the sides.

bake in oven for 1 hour, until potatoes are tender and the top layer is golden brown.

SERVES SIX

red **and yellow capsicum rolls**

Do this whenever both red and yellow capsicums are in season, because the colours are as magical as the flavours. Grazie, Maria Battaglia and Verona, Italy for the ideas.

3 red capsicums

3 yellow capsicums

½ cup dry breadcrumbs

½ cup fetta cheese

3 anchovy fillets, rinsed and finely chopped

1 tablespoon small capers

2 tablespoons pine nuts, roughly chopped

2 tablespoons finely chopped flat-leaf parsley

Freshly ground pepper

3 tablespoons extra virgin olive oil

Fresh basil leaves

roast capsicum over a gas flame or under the grill, turning frequently until charred.

place in a covered bowl for 10 minutes to loosen the skins.

peel, cut in half, remove seeds and trim into 12 neatish rectangles.

mix all remaining ingredients.

place a tablespoon of mixture on each half pepper and roll up.

trim ends, and place rolls side by side, alternating colours, on a serving dish.

serve at room temperature with basil leaves, or warm in a lightly oiled baking dish at 180°C (350°F) for 15 minutes.

SERVES SIX

red and yellow
capsicum rolls

pumpkin **and coconut curry**

A glowing golden pumpkin bowl of pumpkin,
fragrant with fennel seeds and curry leaves.
Serve with simply grilled meats, roast chicken,
or just a glass of wine.

2 tablespoons vegetable oil

1 onion, finely chopped

2.5 cm (1 in) fresh ginger, grated

1 garlic clove

½ teaspoon fennel seeds

4 curry leaves

2 fresh red chillies, chopped

450 grams (1 pound) pumpkin, skinned and
   deseeded

½ teaspoon mustard seeds

1 teaspoon turmeric

½ cup coconut milk

1 cup water

Salt

Coriander leaves for garnish

heat oil and fry onion, ginger, garlic, fennel seeds, curry leaves and chillies, until onion is soft and golden.

cut pumpkin into cubes and add to pan with mustard seeds and turmeric.

fry for 2 minutes, then lower heat and add coconut milk and water.

cook uncovered for 15 minutes or until pumpkin is tender.

add salt to taste.

SERVES TWO TO FOUR

spinach **with raisins and pine nuts**

Who needs fast food when you can do a short
and snappy, glossy-green spinach dish like this?
Team with grilled chicken, lamb or fish.

Bunch of fresh spinach

1 tablespoon pine nuts

Salt

½ cup raisins

Dash of olive oil

Dash of lemon juice

clean spinach thoroughly under plenty of cold running water.

grill pine nuts until golden brown, watching carefully.

bring a pot of salted water to the boil, and toss in raisins and spinach.

drain as soon as spinach goes limp.

toss in olive oil and lemon juice, and scatter with grilled pine nuts.

SERVES FOUR

hot **beetroot salad with fetta**

We are in danger of losing this brilliant, health-giving vegetable altogether unless a new generation gets excited about it. This hot salad is yummy enough to do the job.

Bunch of baby beetroots
Olive oil
Juice of ½ a lemon
2 tablespoons fetta cheese
2 tablespoons walnuts
Freshly ground pepper

scrub beetroots, and cut the stems, leaving 5 cm (2 in) or so of the stalk.

drizzle with a little olive oil and bake at 180°C (350°F) for 30 minutes, until tender when pierced with a fork.

rub off skin under cold running water, leaving stalks.

toss beetroots in a little olive oil and lemon juice and keep warm.

clean leaves and cook in simmering, salted water for a few minutes until limp.

drain leaves and toss in a little olive oil, lemon juice and pepper.

arrange leaves on serving plate and top with baby beets tossed in a little olive oil and vinegar.

crumble cheese and walnuts on top. Serve hot, or at room temperature.

SERVES FOUR

cabbage **with cumin seed**

The much-maligned cabbage gets star treatment that makes it both easy and delicious. Serve with grilled sausages, pork, veal or with your favourite vegetable curry.

1 medium green cabbage
2 tablespoons extra virgin olive oil
1 teaspoon cumin seed
1 teaspoon ground cumin
½ teaspoon sea salt

trim the outer leaves from the cabbage, and shred remaining cabbage finely.

heat oil in a heavy based saucepan, add cumin seed and fry for one minute.

add cabbage, ground cumin and salt, and toss well.

cover pan, and cook over very low heat for 20 to 30 minutes, tossing occasionally, allowing the cabbage to virtually steam.

SERVES FOUR

roasted *and grilled vegetables with prosciutto*

Once you're hooked on crisp, roasted vegetables and juicy grilled vegetables strewn with herbs, you'll never boil anything again. There are no strict measurements with this recipe, so just do as much or as little as you feel like.

To roast

Sweet potatoes, potatoes, parsnip, pumpkin, tomatoes or small onions

4 garlic cloves, smashed

Extra virgin olive oil

Fresh rosemary and oregano

To grill

Eggplant, zucchini, mushrooms or capsicums

Extra virgin olive oil

2 garlic cloves, smashed

Fresh basil and parsley

Salt and freshly ground pepper

8 slices of prosciutto

peel and chop vegetables for roasting, toss in oil and strew with herbs.

roast in a 200°C (400°F) oven for 1 hour or until cooked.

peel and slice vegetables for grilling, and toss in oil, garlic and herbs.

grill vegetables, turning occasionally and basting with remaining olive oil.

arrange on serving plates.

roll prosciutto and tuck into vegetables with fresh herbs.

SERVES FOUR

chinese *cabbage with garlic and ginger*

A visit to an Asian food store will unearth a magical variety of cabbages. Most — Chinese flowering cabbage (choi sum), white cabbage (bak choi), Chinese kale (gai laan), Swatow mustard cabbage (dai gai choi), and Peking cabbage (wong nga bak) — can simply be blanched for a few seconds before being tossed in a stir fry.

1 Chinese cabbage

2 tablespoons peanut oil

1 slice fresh ginger

1 garlic clove, smashed

1 tablespoon chicken stock or water

1 tablespoon dry sherry or rice wine

1 teaspoon light soy sauce

wash and clean cabbage and chop it into 8 cm (3 in) sections, dividing stems from leaves.

plunge stems and thicker leaves into boiling water for up to 2 minutes, and refresh under cold running water.

heat wok, add oil and heat through.

add ginger and garlic and fry to flavour oil, before discarding.

toss stems into oil, and stir fry until they start to soften.

add chicken stock or water, dry sherry or rice wine, then add cabbage, stirring and tossing until the leaves wilt.

splash in the soy, stir through and serve.

SERVES FOUR

spinach **with parmigiano**

Nothing could be simpler than green spinach wilted in a little butter and tossed with nutmeg and cheese. For a complete meal, toss it through some hot orecchiette or farfalle pasta.

2 tablespoons butter

1 kilo (2 pounds) spinach, well washed

Salt and freshly ground pepper

½ teaspoon nutmeg

2 tablespoons grated parmigiano

heat pan, melt butter and add spinach.
cook, tossing, for 3 to 4 minutes.
add salt, pepper, nutmeg and cheese, toss and serve.

SERVES FOUR

zucchini **in herbed olive oil**

A colourful mosaic of diced vegetables at its most beautiful when scattered over or under grilled fish, surrounding roast chicken, or even spooned into a creamy soup.

2 tablespoons olive oil

4 sprigs fresh thyme

1 onion, finely chopped

2 red capsicums

6 green zucchini

6 yellow zucchini

heat oil and thyme together, add onion, and cook until onion is soft and pale.
core and deseed capsicums.
cut capsicums and zucchini into very small dice, add to onion and cook, stirring gently, for 10 minutes.

SERVES SIX

zucchini in
herbed olive oil

cauliflower **with spiced tomato crown**

A spectacular vegetable dish adapted from The Art of Indian Vegetarian Cooking *by Yamuna Devi.*

1 cauliflower

350 gram (12 ounce) can tomatoes

1 bay leaf

6 to 8 peppercorns

1 tablespoon vegetable oil

½ teaspoon ground cumin

½ teaspoon ground coriander

Pinch of cayenne pepper or paprika

½ teaspoon turmeric

½ teaspoon salt

½ teaspoon brown sugar

trim cauliflower, and cook gently in simmering, salted water, stem end down, until tender, but firm (10 to 15 minutes).

gently transfer to a serving platter, cover with foil, and keep warm.

heat tomatoes with bay leaf and peppercorns, cook for 10 minutes, and strain.

heat oil in frypan, add spices and fry for a minute or two.

add tomatoes, salt and sugar, bring to the boil, and continue to cook until thick enough to coat a wooden spoon.

spoon sauce over cauliflower, and serve at the table, cutting into wedges.

SERVES FOUR TO SIX

cauliflower with spiced tomato crown

The female breast is a symbol of food, of a mother's love, of nurturing, of protection, of innocence — and of sheer, rampant, joyous, passionate sex.

Men raised on their mother's milk find it hard to separate food from love, and love from sex. Women, of course, see food as another way to nurture, protect and caress.

Aphrodisiacs, as a concept, were invented by men. The idea of special foods endowing the male of the species with special properties is a very masculine idea, seemingly born of ego and insecurity. Women are more likely to allow mother nature to provide the sensuality: a fresh peach, a floral wine, a delicate fish.

Besides, most allegedly aphrodisiac foods are hard to find (bull's penis), environmentally unacceptable (powdered deer horn), or just plain revolting (snake bile).

There is no doubt, however, that food can set a mood. So let us create our own modern seduction technology, with the sexiest dish in the world, a golden platter of warmed oysters in a slinky champagne sauce resting on a bed of angelhair pasta. Casanova used to eat at least fifty oysters a day for breakfast before he even looked for anyone to seduce. As for caviar, add up the phosphorous, calcium, protein and massive vitamin content, and it's as good for you as powdered deer horn.

The next course could be asparagus, a diuretic which irritates the urinary tract and supposedly excites surrounding areas. The Romans even had a bedroom saying, 'do it quicker than you can cook asparagus', but asparagus is better when quickly cooked, which doesn't augur well for Roman staying power.

Next, choose from radishes, which were eaten with honey by ancient Egyptians before going to bed; sweet potatoes, the aphrodisiacs of the American Indians; lettuce, which was served in any self-respecting German brothel for its recuperative powers, and even garlic, although only if you both have it.

Dessert must be chocolate, declared by a royal physician in seventeenth-century England to be 'provocative to lust'. Even modern chemists admit it contains caffeine and theobromine, both of which stimulate the central nervous system, and phenylethylamine, similar to amphetamines. What more could you want?

Just remember, however, that your mood is even more important than your food. If you are feeling warm, relaxed, happy and loved, then cheese on toast and a nice cup of tea are going to work just as well.

The sexiest dish in the world

Oysters with angelhair pasta and caviar was created by Marco Pierre White, of Harvey's restaurant in London, a rakish, rebellious individual often labelled the sexiest chef in the world.

I've simplified it somewhat, considering you may not have your mind fully on the job at hand:

Take ten fresh oysters and strain their juices into a bowl. Cut some cucumber into very fine strips. Cook a few finely chopped shallots in a little butter, add a few spoonfuls of fish stock and any oyster juices, and boil until reduced by half. Add a touch of cream and keep warm. Arrange warmed oyster shells on a bed of watercress. Cook very fine Cipriani tagliolini pasta until tender. Warm the oysters in the sauce, and spoon into the oyster shells, toppping with cucumber strips and some (real) caviar. This serves two, naturally.

n e w

D I N N E R S

soy chicken
with bak choi
RECIPE 108

You may not read this, because you don't have the time.

Nor do you have the time to cook long, slow casseroles and bake your own bread. You don't have time to fiddle about with tricky dinner party recipes, or try exotic new dishes every day of the week.

In spite of our refrigerators, dishwashers, high-speed kettles, sandwich makers and microwave ovens, we still don't seem to be able to **sit around with our feet up** until ten minutes before dinner.

The truth is, dinner at home is bliss if you want to cook, and hell if you have to cook. Wanna-cooks waltz around the kitchen, humming and sipping wine as they toss together their latest stir fry, while have-to-cooks, well, they just have to.

So how do you turn a have-to-cook into a wanna-cook? You start with terrific produce, because you have to do less to it. Fresh fruits and vegetables come in their own packaging, and can be left in it. A fresh fish needs little gilding. **No mess, no fuss**, and it's on the table before you have time to pour yourself a glass of white wine.

If you simply don't have time to cook the sort of food you like during the week, then cook it on **the weekend**. Do a big, hearty soup on Sunday that will keep you going all week. Make up a few curry pastes when you get back from shopping, and dip into them for days afterwards. Or cook up minced veal and chicken with onions, carrots, tomatoes and herbs, and turn it into a pasta dish one night and a pie the next.

In this way, you can have **fast-lane living** without collision or compromise, and with respect for your body and yourself. It also helps to exploit **high-tech tools** like non-stick pans, and to harness low-tech skills like grilling and snappy stir frying. The time spent becomes much more pleasant if we can involve **friends and family** in the planning and cooking processes, sharing responsibility and pride, and passing on valuable coming-of-age rites like how to **peel an onion**.

Above all, we should generally enjoy the hell out of ourselves. Food that has been a joy to cook is a joy to eat.

fish with a
lemon chilli
crust
RECIPE 106

105

fish **with a lemon chilli crust**

Fresh fish (try flounder, whiting, baby schnapper) is quickly flash-fried with a chunky crumb crust made fragrant with lemon rind. Homemade breadcrumbs are best (see New Basics, page 212).

1 cup breadcrumbs

1 tablespoon finely chopped parsley

½ red chilli, finely chopped

Grated rind of 1 small lemon

2 small, fresh, whole fish, well cleaned

1 free range egg, beaten

1 tablespoon olive oil

1 tablespoon butter

mix breadcrumbs with parsley, chilli and lemon rind.

lay fish into beaten egg on both sides, then press gently into breadcrumbs until coated on both sides.

heat olive oil and butter in a heavy based frypan until hot, and cook until golden brown on both sides, turning carefully once.

SERVES TWO

greek **lamb with beetroot greens**

The gutsy, bold flavours of Greece combined with the tenderness of lamb. Choose firm, small beetroots with fresh-looking stems and leaves, and use the beetroots themselves as an accompanying vegetable.

1 garlic clove

4 well trimmed four-bone racks of lamb

Juice of 1 lemon

Dried oregano

1 tablespoon olive oil

Fresh oregano

Green leaves and stems from a bunch of beetroot

Freshly ground pepper

rub a cut garlic clove over the racks of lamb, drizzle with lemon juice, and press into a plate of dried oregano.

heat olive oil in a heavy based pan, and quickly sear the meat until brown.

bake at 200°C (400°F) for 10 to 15 minutes, and allow to rest in a warm place.

boil cleaned beetroot greens in salted, simmering water for 5 minutes.

drain and dress greens with a little olive oil, lemon juice and pepper.

serve with racks of lamb, fresh oregano, and a squeeze of lemon juice.

SERVES FOUR

greek lamb with
beetroot greens

soy chicken with bak choi

A tantalising Asian marinade becomes the sauce for this quick-smart chicken recipe. You'll find baby or Shanghai bak choi cabbage at your local Asian food store.

6 bak choi cabbages

2 tablespoons soy sauce

2 tablespoons mirin

1 red chilli, chopped

4 trimmed, skinless chicken breasts

3 tablespoons peanut oil

1 extra tablespoon peanut oil

soak cabbages upside down in a bowl of water to loosen any dirt.

cook for 1 minute in simmering, salted water, and drain.

cut cabbages into quarters lengthwise.

combine soy sauce, mirin and chilli, and coat chicken breasts with mixture.

heat peanut oil in a heavy bottomed fry-pan, and sear chicken breasts over high heat for 3 minutes.

turn once, add remaining marinade, and cook until flesh springs back to the touch.

remove chicken and allow to rest.

add remaining peanut oil to the pan juices, toss in cabbage and stir fry for 3 minutes.

slice chicken breast and serve with cabbage, drizzled with pan juices.

SERVES FOUR

cheese gnocchi

A light and fluffy heaven-sent dish known and loved in Italy as gnocchi alla Romana. You can make it days ahead and freeze, prior to the final cooking.

4 cups milk

Pinch of grated nutmeg

1 cup Italian semolina

Salt

2 egg yolks, lightly beaten

1 tablespoon melted butter

1 cup grated parmigiano

1 extra teaspoon butter

bring milk and nutmeg to the boil.

reduce heat, and add semolina gradually, whisking continually to avoid lumps.

cook for 10 to 15 minutes over low heat, whisking continually until the mixture is thick and sticks to the whisk.

remove pan from heat, and beat in salt, egg yolks, butter, and all but a tablespoon of the cheese.

spread mixture onto an oiled baking tray and smooth it with a wet spatula knife until 1 cm (½ in) thick.

chill for 2 hours, or freeze.

cut semolina into rounds or triangles, and arrange in a lightly oiled baking dish, over-lapping each other slightly.

dot with extra butter, and sprinkle with remaining cheese.

bake at 200°C (400°F) for 10 to 15 minutes until golden and fluffy.

SERVES SIX

red **roast duck curry**

You can cheat your way into a decent roast duck curry by getting a barbecued duck from Chinatown, and using canned curry paste and coconut milk. It's not how they do it in Thailand, but this isn't Thailand.

1 lemon grass stalk

1 cup coconut milk

1 tablespoon Maesri red curry paste

1 red chilli, split and deseeded

1 Chinese roast duckling

½ cup water

2 kaffir lime leaves

1 teaspoon sugar

1 red capsicum, deseeded and chopped into squares

2 green zucchini, chopped into small cubes

2 yellow zucchini, chopped into small cubes

Few sprigs of coriander, chopped

peel lemon grass, and slice tender white part of stem into fine rings.

scoop the thick cream from the top of the coconut milk, and heat it in a wok or fry-pan with curry paste, chilli and lemon grass.

simmer for 10 minutes until it starts to smell wonderful.

remove breasts from duck and chop into 4 rectangles.

remove legs, and chop into 2.

add duck, remaining coconut milk, water, kaffir lime leaves, sugar, capsicum and zucchini to sauce, and cook over medium heat for 10 minutes, until vegetables are cooked.

add coriander and serve with jasmine rice.

SERVES FOUR

pasta **with lentils and yoghurt**

A Mod Med dish that will knock your socks off with its rich creamy lentil sauce. A good example of how yoghurt can replace cream and win hands down.

1 cup brown lentils

4 cups water or chicken stock

1 bay leaf

2 tablespoons olive oil

2 onions, chopped

1 garlic clove, crushed

1 teaspoon coriander, ground

1 teaspoon cumin, ground

Pinch of cayenne pepper

Salt and freshly ground pepper

2 tablespoons tomato passato

100 grams (4 ounces) spaghettini per person

3 tablespoons plain natural yoghurt

Coriander and flat-leaf parsley

combine lentils, bay leaf, and water or stock, and bring to boil.

simmer for 20 minutes or until tender.

heat olive oil and cook onions until soft and golden.

add garlic, spices, salt and drained lentils.

add tomato passato and enough lentil water to make a sauce.

keep sauce warm.

cook pasta in lots of boiling, salted water until tender but firm to the bite.

drain and toss pasta in lentils.

stir in yoghurt, top with coriander and parsley and serve.

SERVES FOUR

crab, chilli and garlic pasta

An easy and impressive dish that makes a little crab go a long way.

4 sand or blue swimmer crabs, cooked or uncooked

100 grams (4 ounces) spaghettini or linguine per person

3 tablespoons olive oil

1 chilli, finely chopped

2 garlic cloves, peeled and bruised

Smidge of butter

2 tablespoons chopped parsley

Freshly ground pepper

drown live crabs in cold fresh water for an hour or two.

cook in plenty of boiling, salted water for 8 to 10 minutes.

use a knife to lever the shell from the rear, and clean fronds away.

break each crab into 4, and crack legs, reserving shell and some legs for garnish, and set aside flesh.

cook pasta in plenty of boiling, salted water until cooked but still firm.

heat olive oil, chilli and garlic in a pan.

add crab flesh and legs, and toss gently to heat through, then add drained pasta.

serve with butter and lots of parsley and pepper.

top with crab shell, warmed in a bowl of hot water.

SERVES FOUR

lion's head meatballs

My attempt to match the silken smooth lion's head meatballs of the Shanghai Hotel, Shanghai, so-called because of their supposed resemblance to the head of the noble lion, with the cabbage forming the mane.

700 grams (1½ pounds) minced pork

3 spring onions, chopped

2 slices of ginger, finely chopped

1 tablespoon cornflour

1 tablespoon Chinese rice wine or dry sherry

Salt

2 tablespoons peanut oil

4 small bak choi cabbages

2 cups chicken stock

place pork, spring onions, ginger, cornflour, wine and salt in food processor and blend until smooth.

shape by hand into meatballs of a generous size.

roll in a little extra cornflour.

heat oil and fry meatballs until golden.

clean cabbages, and cut in half lengthwise.

add cabbage and chicken stock to meatballs, and bring to boil.

cover, reduce heat and cook gently for 40 minutes.

serve with steamed rice.

SERVES SIX

seared **lamb with garlicky white bean purée**

Beautiful Australian lamb (you can tell my father is a sheep farmer) tastes even better when married with garlic, rosemary and white beans.

3 small rolled loins of lamb

4 garlic cloves, smashed

2 tablespoons rosemary leaves

½ cup olive oil

2 cups white cannellini beans

Salt and freshly ground pepper

½ teaspoon paprika

1 tablespoon lemon juice

soak beans in cold water overnight.

trim lamb of any fat, and marinate with garlic, rosemary and olive oil overnight.

drain beans, place in pot, cover in cold water, bring to the boil, and cook gently for 1 hour or until tender.

heat a heavy bottomed pan and sear the lamb for 2 or 3 minutes to seal juices.

roast lamb at 180°C (350°F) for 15 minutes, then turn oven off and allow to rest for 10 minutes.

drain beans, place in food processor with marinade, and whizz.

heat beans, and add salt, pepper, paprika and lemon juice.

slice lamb thickly, and place slices on a bed of warm white bean purée.

tuck fresh sprigs of rosemary between slices and serve.

SERVES SIX

lemon **chicken with olives**

A sunny Moroccan chicken dish, exotically flavoured with saffron, spices, preserved lemons and olives. Serve with a big bowl of couscous.

1 free range chicken

½ teaspoon salt

1 tablespoon peanut oil

2 large onions, grated

2 garlic cloves, crushed

1 teaspoon ginger

1 teaspoon hot paprika

1½ teaspoons cinnamon or 1 cinnamon stick

Big pinch of saffron powder

2 cups water

2 preserved lemons (see New Basics, page 208)

20 kalamata olives

1 to 2 tablespoons lemon juice

Salt and freshly ground pepper

clean chicken and rub inside and out with salt.

heat oil in a heavy bottomed casserole, add chicken and brown lightly on all sides.

add onion, garlic, spices, and water, and cook over a low heat for 40 minutes, turning chicken occasionally and adding more water if necessary.

rinse preserved lemons, and discard flesh.

add lemons and olives and cook for the last 5 minutes.

add lemon juice, salt and pepper to taste.

place chicken on a large, warm serving plate, strain sauce on top, tuck in lemons and olives, and serve with couscous.

SERVES FOUR

lamb and fresh mint curry

A tender lamb curry adapted from Madhur Jaffrey's 'do piaza', blasted at the last minute with mint, lemon juice and chilli.

450 grams (1 pound) boned meat from lamb
   shoulder, cut into 2.5 cm (1 in) cubes

3 onions, sliced into fine rings

½ teaspoon salt

¼ teaspoon cayenne pepper

1 teaspoon grated ginger

1 garlic clove, crushed

½ teaspoon ground turmeric

2 tablespoons vegetable oil

2 tablespoons coriander leaves

3 tablespoons mint leaves

1 fresh green chilli, chopped

2 tablespoons lemon juice

combine meat, onions, salt, cayenne, ginger, garlic, turmeric, vegetable oil and 2 cups of water in a heavy frypan.

bring to a simmer, cover, lower the heat and cook gently for 2 or 3 hours.

blend mint, coriander, chilli and lemon juice in food processor until smooth.

add herbs and simmer for the last few minutes.

serve with steamed rice.

SERVES FOUR

roasted fish with herbs

Colourful, dramatic and drop-dead easy fish encrusted with fresh herbs.

1 cup flat-leaf parsley leaves

1 cup chervil

1 cup basil leaves

2 tablespoons virgin olive oil

1 cup torn white bread

Salt and freshly ground pepper

6 thick fillets of firm white deep sea fish,
   skinned

chop herbs finely with a sharp knife.

add olive oil, bread, salt and pepper, and mix well.

spread paste on top side of each fillet, and chill for at least an hour.

place fillets on a preheated baking pan and bake at 200°C (400°F) for 6 to 8 minutes, depending on thickness. The fish should still be moist in the centre.

slide fish under a preheated griller for 2 minutes until the topping forms a crust.

SERVES SIX

risotto **with lemon and parmigiano**

This is a gorgeous dish on its own, or a sophisticated accompaniment to grilled or roasted meats, or long, slow-cooked oxtail.

1 tablespoon olive oil

1 tablespoon butter

1 onion, peeled and finely chopped

2 cups Italian arborio rice

4 cups chicken stock

½ teaspoon saffron powder, or a few saffron strands

Salt and freshly ground pepper

Juice of ½ a large lemon

½ cup grated parmigiano

Grated rind of 1 lemon

heat oil and butter in a heavy bottomed saucepan over medium heat.

add onion and rice, and cook for a few minutes, stirring with a wooden spoon.

add boiling stock and saffron, and stir gently.

cover, adjust heat and simmer quietly for 20 minutes or so, stirring occasionally until liquid is almost absorbed, and rice is tender.

remove from heat, and stir in lemon juice, cheese, lemon rind, salt and pepper.

return to heat and cook for 1 minute, stirring, before serving.

S E R V E S   F O U R

chicken **with lots of garlic**

Yes, lots. This aromatic Provençal dish cooks the garlic to a soft purée that is sweet, nutty and socially acceptable the morning after.

1 large free range chicken

Salt

1 bay leaf

2 tablespoons virgin olive oil

40 garlic cloves, unpeeled

A few rosemary, thyme, sage or parsley leaves

2 celery stalks, chopped

2 red or orange capsicums, chopped

Freshly ground pepper

½ cup white wine

1 cup chicken stock

2 tablespoons flour

1 tablespoon water

4 slices of bread

remove fat from just inside cavity, and rub chicken with a little salt.

pop bay leaf inside.

heat oil in a large casserole.

add garlic, herbs, celery, capsicums and pepper, and cook for 5 minutes.

add wine and chicken stock, bring to boil and simmer for 3 minutes.

add chicken, turning to coat in sauce, cover with a tight-fitting lid, and seal edges with a flour and water paste.

bake at 180°C (350°F) for 1 hour.

break seal and transfer to a warm platter.

grill bread, and serve with chicken so that garlic can be squeezed onto toast and dipped into the juices.

S E R V E S   F O U R

new DESSERTS

chocolate bread
and butter
pudding
RECIPE 126

Natural healing methods tend to concentrate on herbal concoctions, relaxation techniques, and meditation. While these methods do seem to have **beneficial effects** on those who practise them, there is one other thing that can reduce stress and instantly create a general feeling of warmth and well-being.

A great dessert.

From a sophisticated fruit jelly to a mother-lovely sticky toffee pudding, dessert is still a small and special visit to the past, to that time of **innocence** before we knew how to spell kilojoule or cholesterol.

For a dessert that won't turn you into a plump pudding, harvest the fruits of the season and reap the benefits. **Sun-ripened** figs and juicy black cherries, plump downy peaches and punnets of berries need very little done to them.

Cut a slice of crisp, **chilled watermelon** to take the heat out of the hottest day, or peel and bite a fresh lychee that has never seen a can. Marinate strawberries in a little sugar and raspberry vinegar (yes, *vinegar*). **Poach a perfect pear** in sauternes, a peach in champagne, or soup up a fruit salad with ginger and lemon grass.

In winter, give yourself permission to **regress** to childhood with grandmotherly favourites given a new lease of life. Bread and butter pudding grows up with the addition of lemon zest and chocolate. Ice-cream and jelly is an adult treat when the jelly is made with Campari and orange juice. And, of course, decidedly, unquestionably and incontestably, you can have your **chocolate cake** and eat it too.

The luscious sweetness and the honey and treacle aromas of a dessert wine can also make a perfect dessert in a glass, when served with bone-dry Italian sweet biscuits for dipping and sipping.

No matter how healthy your diet, there is no need to punish yourself by banning all sweet things as wicked or sinful. Instead, treat them as **small pleasures**, share them willingly, put them into perspective, and then curl up like a cat with a bowl of cream and **enjoy yourself**. The world will suddenly seem a much nicer place. And you won't burn in hell forevermore, unless you **eat the whole lot**.

a very beautiful
pear tart
RECIPE 120

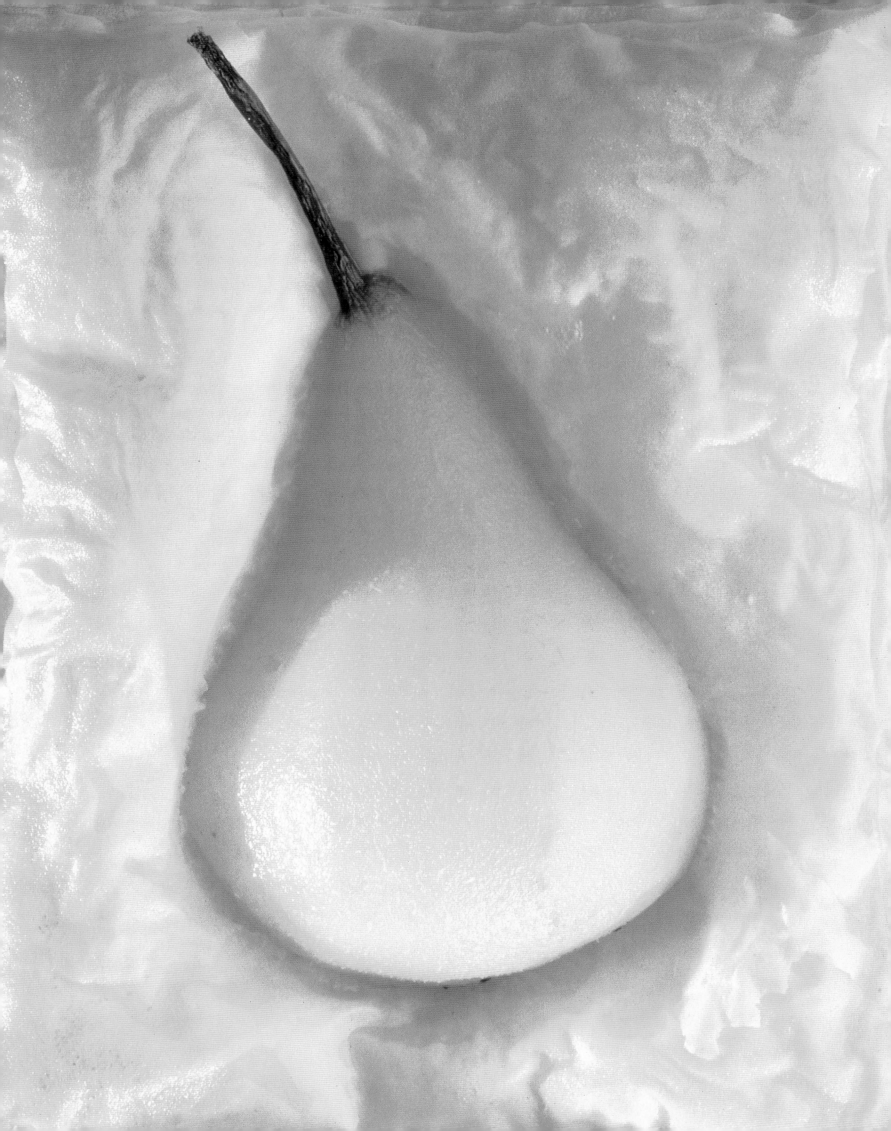

a **very beautiful pear tart**

Sweet poached pears on no-fuss filo pastry make a fast and fabulous finish. Serve with vanilla custard (see New Basics, page 219).

1 bottle sweet dessert wine

3 tablespoons castor sugar

3 firm brown-skinned pears

2 cloves

1 cinnamon stick

1 vanilla bean, split lengthwise

1 packet of filo pastry

3 tablespoons melted butter or sweet almond oil

bring wine and sugar to the boil, stirring.

peel pears, and place upright in liquid with cloves, cinnamon and vanilla bean.

simmer for 10 to 15 minutes or until tender.

leave pears to cool, then drain and cut in half, retaining stem and removing core.

unfold filo pastry, and cover with a damp cloth while working.

brush 1 sheet with butter or almond oil. Working quickly, place another sheet on top of it, and brush with butter, repeating process until you have 8 sheets. Cut in half to form 2 squares.

repeat process until you have 6 squares.

place half a pear on each square, and trim pastry.

brush with remaining butter or oil and bake for 10 to 15 minutes until the pastry puffs and turns golden.

drizzle a little of the poaching liquid on top of pear to serve.

MAKES SIX

fruit **salad soup**

Fresh fruits float in a sweet tangy syrup, fragrant with ginger and lemon grass. It's as cool as a cucumber, or it would be if cucumber were a fruit.

Rind of 1 orange and 1 lemon, cut into tiny strips

1 bottle sweet dessert wine

2 cups cold water

2 tablespoons castor sugar

1 vanilla bean, split lengthwise

1 tablespoon grated ginger

2 lemon grass stalks

5 cloves

20 fresh mint leaves

4 passionfruit

Pineapple, mango, peach, papaya, kiwi fruit, banana, strawberries and other berries

Extra mint leaves

bring all ingredients other than fruit to the boil and simmer for 30 minutes.

cover and cool before chilling overnight.

remove pulp from passionfruit, push it through a sieve, and add juice to syrup.

peel and cut fruit into cubes, and arrange in chilled soup plates with berries, tucking extra mint leaves into fruit.

strain syrup and spoon over fruit until it just starts to float.

sprinkle with a few reserved pieces of lemon grass and orange and lemon rind from the syrup, and serve.

SERVES FOUR

fruit salad soup

apple **berry tart**

A berry-spattered fruit tart on crisp filo pastry that takes ten minutes to make and ten minutes to bake.

1 packet of filo pastry

3 tablespoons melted butter or sweet nut oil

2 Granny Smith apples

1 cup raspberries

1 tablespoon sugar

unroll filo pastry, and cover with a damp cloth while working.

brush 1 sheet with butter or oil, place another sheet on top, and brush it with butter or oil.

repeat until you have 8 layers.

cut into 4 squares or rectangles.

peel and core apples, slice incredibly thinly, and layer slices on pastry.

dot with raspberries, brush with butter, scatter with sugar, and bake on a non-stick tray at 180°C (350°F) for 10 or 15 minutes until golden.

SERVES FOUR

chargrilled **fruits with champagne froth**

A frothy, light, champagne-scented sabayon sauce that makes the most of quickly grilled summer fruits.

Assorted fruits: peach, plum, apricot, papaya, mango, or berries

2 tablespoons brown sugar

3 egg yolks

3 tablespoons castor sugar

3 tablespoons sparkling or still white wine

peel, stone or slice fruits into appropriate pieces ready for eating.

place under a hot grill and sprinkle with brown sugar.

watch carefully as the sugar melts and caramelises on the fruit.

whisk yolks, sugar and wine in a heat-proof bowl until pale.

place bowl over a pot of simmering water, and continue to whisk, or beat with a hand-held electric mixer, over heat for 10 or 15 minutes, until thick, light and fluffy.

arrange grilled fruits on serving plates and surround with spoonfuls of frothy champagne sauce.

SERVES FOUR

warm *berries*

The gentle heat intensifies the flavour of fresh berries. Serve with a slice of chocolate cake, spoon over a warm stack of paper thin crêpes, or with a freshly poached pear.

3 tablespoons sugar

½ cup water

1 tablespoon lemon juice

3 punnets of berries: strawberries (halved), blueberries, or blackberries or mixed

heat sugar and water in a heavy pan and stir until dissolved.

add lemon juice and all berries and cook gently for no more than 2 or 3 minutes, shaking pan gently to coat them with syrup.

remove from heat and serve warm, or allow to cool.

SERVES FOUR TO SIX

fruit sushi

fruit *sushi*

This is one of those silly ideas that actually work, because the combination of fresh fruit and coconut rice is so delicious. The idea first surfaced at the Hyatt Regency Hotel in Singapore.

300 grams (11 ounces) white rice

300 millilitres (11 fluid ounces) cold water

3 tablespoons coconut milk

2 tablespoons sugar

1 tablespoon coconut liqueur

Fresh fruit in season, sliced thinly (strawberry, kiwifruit, apricot)

1 cup raspberries

1 tablespoon sugar

rinse rice under cold running water until water runs clear, not cloudy.

bring rice and cold water to the boil, then cover, turn heat to very low, and cook for 15 minutes, until rice is tender and has absorbed all the water.

transfer to bowl, add coconut milk, sugar, and liqueur, and mix gently as rice cools.

form rice into sushi logs by pressing between damp hands.

blend raspberries with sugar in blender and strain.

arrange the fresh fruit on top of each rice log, and serve with raspberry dipping sauce.

SERVES FOUR

little **apple turnups**

They're cute, they're delicious, and they're easy. Make the quick shortcrust pastry here or buy it from a good pastry shop.

1 quantity quick shortcrust pastry (see New Basics, page 219)

4 golden delicious or Granny Smith apples

60 grams (2 ounces) unsalted butter

2 tablespoons light brown sugar

1 free range egg, beaten

preheat oven to 220°C (425°F).

divide chilled pastry into 4, and roll each piece until it forms a circle of 15 cm (6 in) diameter.

place pastry rounds on a lightly-oiled baking sheet.

peel and core the apples.

cut each apple into 12 even wedges.

melt butter in a heavy bottomed pan over medium high heat, add apples and sugar, and cook for around 15 minutes until lightly browned.

place apples in the centre of each pastry round.

fold the edges of the dough over the apples to form a 2.5 cm (1 in) border, and brush with beaten egg.

bake for about 20 minutes until golden.

serve warm or at room temperature.

SERVES FOUR

grilled **figs with cinnamon mascarpone**

If figs aren't available, poach pears in sauternes until just tender, and use instead. Drizzle with a little poaching syrup before topping with mascarpone and cinnamon.

12 firm, ripe figs

4 tablespoons honey

1 cup mascarpone

1 teaspoon cinnamon

wash and dry figs, and cut in half.

place figs cut side up in a shallow, buttered baking dish.

pour honey over figs from a warm spoon.

grill until figs soften and heat through.

serve warm, topped with mascarpone and a dusting of cinnamon.

SERVES SIX

little apple
turnups

chocolate **bread and butter pudding**

There is only one way to improve a sweet, rich, fluffed-up, fruity bread and butter pudding, and that is to add chocolate.

2 tablespoons sultanas

2 tablespoons liqueur (e.g. Cointreau)

1 skinny French breadstick or plain white sliced bread

2 tablespoons soft butter

2 tablespoons dark chocolate, grated

2 cups milk

¾ cup cream

1 vanilla bean, split lengthwise

4 free range eggs

½ cup sugar

soak sultanas in liqueur for 1 hour.

cut breadstick into very thin slices, or fresh bread into triangles, and butter lightly.

arrange bread in a buttered ovenproof dish, and scatter sultanas and chocolate between each layer.

heat milk, cream and vanilla bean to boiling point.

remove from heat and leave to cool slightly.

beat eggs and sugar together until pale, then add milk, stirring constantly.

pour mixture over bread and leave for 10 minutes to absorb.

bake at 180°C (350°F) for 30 to 40 minutes, until pudding has risen, custard is set and top is golden brown.

SERVES FOUR

sticky **lime pudding**

This is like a soft cake on top, with a tangy lime sauce below. It doesn't matter where you start eating it, it's all equally delicious.

1 tablespoon butter

½ cup sugar

2 tablespoons plain flour, sifted

Juice and grated rind of 2 ripe limes

1 cup milk

2 free range eggs, separated

beat butter and sugar until pale and creamy.

add flour, lime juice and rind.

add milk and egg yolks.

beat egg whites until stiff, and fold into mixture.

pour into a buttered ovenproof dish, and bake at 180°C (350°F) for 20 to 30 minutes until top is golden.

serve warm with lightly whipped cream.

SERVES FOUR

sticky lime pudding

campari and orange jelly

A brilliant tangerine-coloured jelly with an irresistible bite, thanks to the distinctive Italian taste of Campari bitters.

2 cups freshly squeezed orange juice

2 or 3 tablespoons Campari bitters

1 tablespoon powdered gelatine

½ cup boiling water

1 tablespoon castor sugar

strain orange juice of pips and debris, and add Campari until you have a gorgeous tangerine colour.

dissolve gelatine in boiling water, then add castor sugar and stir until dissolved.

pour into one dampened 2-cup jelly mould or 4 individual moulds.

chill for 3 or 4 hours.

dip mould into hot water and gently up-end jelly onto serving plate.

SERVES FOUR

macadamia tart

A gorgeous, gooey nutty tart filled with cholesterol-free macadamia nuts.

1 quantity quick shortcrust pastry (see New Basics, page 219)

300 grams (11 ounces) macadamia nuts

4 free range eggs

1 cup brown sugar

¾ cup corn syrup

3 tablespoons melted butter

1 teaspoon vanilla extract

roll out pastry until thin, and line a buttered 20 cm (8 in) pie dish.

weight with pastry beads or dry beans, and bake at 180°C (350°F) oven until pastry is almost cooked but not browned.

discard beads or beans and fill with macadamia nuts.

beat eggs, and add sugar, corn syrup, butter and vanilla.

mix well and pour over macadamia nuts.

bake at 200°C (400°F) for 10 minutes, then reduce heat to 180°C (350°F) and bake for 40 minutes or until completely set.

cover pastry edge with foil if it browns too quickly.

leave to cool completely in the oven.

SERVES EIGHT

Some flavours aren't interested in settling down to a life of wedded bliss. They just want to go to bed with each other.

Tomato *and* **basil**
Mint *and* **white beans**
Oregano *and* **fetta cheese**
Tarragon *and* **chicken**
Coffee *and* **rum**
Bacon *and* **tomatoes**
Pear *and* **parmigiano**
Fig *and* **prosciutto**
Ham *and* **mustard**
Toast *and* **butter**
Toast *and* **butter** *and* **caviar**
Vodka *and* **cranberry juice**
Draught beer *and* **pickled onions**
Crab *and* **ginger**

Beef *and* **burgundy**
Champagne *and* **anything**
Oysters *and* **caviar**
Tuna *and* **wasabi**
Kangaroo *and* **pinot noir**
Bangers *and* **mash**
Shark fin *and* **cognac**
Quince paste *and* **stracchino**
Salmon *and* **dill**
Dragonwell tea *and* **shrimps**
Yoghurt *and* **honey**
Pheasant *and* **juniper berries**

n e w CAKES

chocolate
beetroot cake
RECIPE 138

Cakes are the edible milestones in our lives. They have always been there, measuring our birthdays, weddings and Christmases in white sugar, rich marzipan, frothy cream and **pink candles**.

Their shapes have changed as our lives have changed: a key for a 21st birthday, a scholar's cap for a graduation, an aeroplane for a first trip overseas. There are cakes for christenings, confirmations, ordinations and anniversaries. And there is always a good cake at a good wake.

You know you have finally, utterly grown up when you can bake a whole cake **just for you** and no one else. In a classic piece of recycling, one is even meant to store away the top tier of one's wedding cake for the first baby's christening party. (And what? The bottom layer for the **divorce** party?)

In Australia, cakes have always ranged from the purely functional (filling up the sheep shearers to keep them going for another two hours) to the highly decorative ('I can do better rolled fondant cover than you can, so there'). But a good cake is so much more than food or fantasy. It's a **necessity of life**, or at the very least, of lifestyle.

We no longer stop for a civilised and leisurely afternoon tea, but a cake still takes the cake for those times when we like to reward ourselves for doing something absolutely brilliant, or to make us **feel better** after doing something absolutely dreadful.

These days, a cake is also seen at the best dinner parties in town. After all, it's easy to make, easy to bake ahead of time, easy to accessorise with fresh fruits or a delicate custard, and it sweeps guests from dessert through to coffee **in a single slice**.

So, let us bake cake. Not gooey cake filled with

artificially induced cream and garishly coloured icing in the form of Garfield, Batman, a football or a female torso. What we need is a good, honest cake full of fresh fruit and fresh free range eggs. And the **odd bit of chocolate**, *please.*

bananarama
cake
RECIPE 138

greek **yoghurt cake**

A traditional cake made velvety with yoghurt and fragrant with lemon.

200 grams (7 ounces) butter

1 cup castor sugar

Grated rind of 1 lemon

4 free range eggs, separated

2 cups plain flour

1 teaspoon baking powder

1 teaspoon bicarbonate of soda

Pinch of salt

1 cup natural yoghurt

heat oven to 180°C (350°F).

cream butter and sugar with lemon rind until pale.

add egg yolks and beat well.

sift dry ingredients together twice.

add some to the mixture, stirring well, then add some of the yoghurt.

repeat process until all flour and yoghurt is combined.

beat egg whites until stiff and peaky, and fold gently into mixture.

pour into a lightly oiled 23 cm (9 in) springform cake tin, or two 15 cm (6 in) springform tins, and bake for 45 to 65 minutes, depending on size, or until an inserted skewer comes out clean.

cool.

dust with icing sugar to serve, or ice with home-made lemon curd (see New Basics, page 210).

SERVES SIX

tiny **passionfruit cakes**

It's time we did something with those glorious purple-skinned fruits that hang over our back fences. These tiny, light cakes are perfect with coffee at the end of a meal.

90 grams (3 ounces) butter

½ cup castor sugar

1 free range egg, plus 1 egg yolk

Pulp of 3 passionfruit

140 grams (5 ounces) self-raising flour, sifted

Icing sugar

cream butter and sugar until pale.

beat in egg and extra yolk until pale and fluffy.

stir in passionfruit pulp.

add flour gradually, then spoon mixture into chocolate truffle-size paper cases until two-thirds full.

bake at 180°C (350°F) for 15 minutes or until golden at the edges.

just before serving, sift a little icing sugar over the top.

MAKES TWENTY

chocolate **beetroot cake**

Yep, beetroot. Like the carrot in a carrot cake, beetroot keeps the cake moist and helps it to last for days. (As if any chocolate cake is going to last for days.) My thanks to Stan Tesch for this.

½ cup cocoa powder

1½ cups plain flour

1½ teaspoons baking powder

Pinch of salt

1½ cups castor sugar

1 cup corn oil

1 teaspoon vanilla essence

3 free range eggs, beaten

1 cup cooked beetroot, puréed

2 tablespoons walnuts, finely chopped

sift cocoa, flour, baking powder and salt.

mix with sugar.

add corn oil, vanilla, eggs, beetroot and walnuts and mix well, until it is a glorious purple colour.

pour into a buttered and floured 18 cm (7 in) round or square pan.

bake at 190°C (375°F) for 50 minutes, or until an inserted skewer comes out clean.

allow to cool before removing from pan.

dust top with icing sugar to serve.

SERVES SIX

bananarama **cake**

Dutch-born cake queen Lilli Hendriksen perfected the theory and philosophy of banana cake while at The Benedykt Café in Melbourne.

300 grams (11 ounces) butter, softened

2 cups brown sugar

4 free range eggs

2 cups banana purée

Rind of 1 lemon

4 cups self-raising flour

1 teaspoon bicarbonate of soda

1 quantity cream cheese icing (see Flowerpot carrot cake, page 142)

8 large or 12 medium bananas

1 packet of Marie biscuits, finely crushed

cream butter and sugar until pale.

beat in eggs, one at a time.

add banana purée and lemon zest and gently stir through.

sift flour and bicarbonate of soda, and fold into mixture.

pour into 2 well-greased 30 cm (12 in) tins.

bake at 180°C (350°F) for 25 minutes or until firm.

allow to cool before unmoulding.

spread icing on the cake and arrange whole bananas in concentric rings.

add enough filling to cover bananas then sandwich other cake on top.

ice sides and top of cake thinly and chill for 2 hours.

roll sides of cake gently in biscuits.

top with remaining icing and a light sprinkling of crushed biscuits.

SERVES TEN

incredibly **wonderful chocolate cake**

The best-ever, no-holds-barred, all-bets-off flourless cake, an Elizabeth David classic that defies reinvention.

250 grams (9 ounces) dark, bitter chocolate

150 grams (5 ounces) castor sugar

150 grams (5 ounces) butter

100 grams (3 ounces) ground almonds

5 free range eggs, separated

Icing sugar

melt chocolate, sugar and butter in a bowl sitting in a pot of simmering water.

remove from heat, stir thoroughly to combine, mix in ground almonds, then beat in the egg yolks one by one.

beat egg whites until stiff and peaky, and stir a couple of spoonfuls into the chocolate mixture to lighten it, before gently folding in the rest.

turn into a buttered and floured 20 cm (8 in) round or square cake tin, and bake at 180°C (350°F) for 40 to 50 minutes.

leave to cool before removing from tin.

dust with icing sugar to serve.

SERVES SIX

upside-down **fruit cake**

A brilliant, perfect-every-time cake with an ever-changing topping (or is that bottom?) of fruit from Australian Gourmet Traveller *magazine. Try it with plums, raspberries, strawberries, prunes or bananas.*

2/3 cup sugar

1/2 cup water

1 cup any fresh fruit

140 grams (5 ounces) butter

1/2 cup castor sugar

3 free range eggs

3/4 cup self-raising flour

1 teaspoon baking powder

2 tablespoons ground almonds

1 tablespoon Cointreau or similar liqueur

melt sugar and water in a small pan over low heat, stirring until sugar dissolves.

boil until syrup turns golden brown.

pour immediately into a lightly oiled 20 cm (8 in) round cake tin, swirling to coat.

lay fruit on caramel.

cream butter and sugar until pale.

add eggs, one at a time, beating well.

sift flour and baking powder, and fold into mixture.

add almonds and liqueur.

pour over fruit and bake at 190°C (375°F) for 45 minutes.

cool slightly, run a knife around the edge, turn out, and serve with cream.

SERVES SIX

upside-down
fruit cake
PHOTO 140

panforte

Is it a cakey biscuit, or a biscuity cake? Italian panforte ('strong bread') is traditionally served at Christmas in Siena, but we can have it with coffee at the end of a meal, anytime.

1 cup glacé fruits (melon, peach, pear, citron)

1 cup dried figs

2 tablespoons good quality cocoa powder

1 teaspoon ground cinnamon

1 pinch ground cloves

1 pinch ground nutmeg

1 cup honey

½ cup castor sugar

1 cup blanched almonds

½ cup roasted hazelnuts

½ cup walnuts

chop fruits roughly, and mix with cocoa powder and spices.

heat honey and sugar in a saucepan, stirring constantly, until a drop of the mixture solidifies when you drop it in a saucer of cold water.

remove from heat and add to fruits and nuts.

mix well, trying desperately to ignore how messy and sticky it is.

line the bottom of a 20 cm (8 in) cake tin with greaseproof paper, and pour mixture on, pressing down lightly.

bake at 180°C (350°F) for 1 hour.

cool before unmoulding, and leave in a cool place overnight.

dust with icing sugar, then cut into bite-size pieces.

SERVES EIGHT

flowerpot **carrot cake**

A rich, fruity and downright yummy carrot cake studded with walnuts and raisins.

2½ cups plain flour

1 tablespoon baking powder

1 tablespoon ground cinnamon

1 teaspoon ground nutmeg

1 teaspoon allspice

2 cups sugar

1½ cups corn oil

4 free range eggs

1 tablespoon vanilla essence

2 cups puréed, cooked carrots

1 cup chopped walnuts

1 cup raisins

Cream cheese icing

½ cup butter

1½ cups cream cheese

½ teaspoon vanilla essence

2 teaspoons lemon juice

1 cup icing sugar

preheat oven to 180°C (350°F).

sift flour, baking powder, cinnamon, nutmeg, allspice and sugar into a bowl.

add corn oil, lightly beaten eggs and vanilla essence and beat well.

fold in carrot purée, walnuts and raisins.

line a 1 litre (1 quart) new terracotta pot (soaked overnight) with greaseproof paper, and pour in mixture.

bake for 1 hour until a skewer inserted in the centre comes out clean.

beat all icing ingredients, and use to ice top or sandwich 2 halves together.

SERVES EIGHT

walnut, apricot and fig torte

One of Melbourne's most famous cakes, this beauty from Café Sweethearts has a crusty meringue outside, and a moist, figgy inside.

9 egg whites, at room temperature

2½ cups brown sugar

1 cup chopped walnuts

1 cup chopped dried apricots

1 cup chopped dried figs

1½ tablespoons cornflour

1 teaspoon vanilla essence

beat egg whites on full speed until stiff and peaky.

add sugar, one cup at a time, still beating, until all sugar is incorporated.

combine nuts, apricots, figs, cornflour and vanilla essence.

fold nut and fruit mixture into egg whites, and pour into a greased and lined 26 cm (10 in) springform pan.

peak the meringue with your fingers.

bake at 150°C (300°F) for around 1½ hours until light brown and fairly firm to touch, then reduce heat to 120°C (250°F) and bake for another 1½ hours.

turn off heat and leave in the oven to cool.

serve with fresh cream or mascarpone.

S E R V E S   E I G H T

spiced apple cake

This is a big, chunky, fruity, spicy cake for a special morning or afternoon tea. I advise you to skip lunch.

1 cup raisins

½ cup rum or brandy

1 cup self-raising flour

1 teaspoon baking powder

½ teaspoon ground nutmeg

½ teaspoon ground cinnamon

½ teaspoon ground ginger

½ teaspoon ground cloves

Pinch of salt

140 grams (5 ounces) butter

1½ cups sugar

3 free range eggs

2 cups chopped, unpeeled apples

1 cup chopped walnuts

soak raisins in rum or brandy.

sift flours, baking powder, spices and salt.

beat butter and sugar until pale and fluffy.

add eggs one at a time, beating after each addition.

fold in flour mixture gradually.

add apples, nuts and drained raisins. If batter is very thick, add half the rum or brandy.

pour into a 25 cm (10 in) pan and bake for 1½ hours at 180°C (350°F) until an inserted skewer comes out clean.

cool and serve.

S E R V E S   E I G H T

If you don't think you have the time to cook an interesting, decent meal every night of the week, then you have been conned. Conned by countless TV commercials for prettily packaged sauces, salsas, chips and dips. Conned by images of viciously slender models sipping nutrasweetened drinks and always getting their guy. Conned by the 11,000 supermarkets of Australia and their 15,000 different items. And quite likely, conned by a male-dominated society into believing that it is the duty of the female to bake the bread as well as to earn it.

So let us dispense with the microwave, just as we discarded the electric frypan, say no to the powdered cappuccino mix, walk past the crap on the supermarket shelves, refuse to buy anything called instant, and embrace the new fast food, before it is too late.

The new fast food is barbecued prawns and fresh apples and antipasto and vegetable soups and snappy stir fries and softly scrambled eggs and chargrilled quail and roasted lemon chicken and grilled lobster sandwiches and calamari and couscous and flourless chocolate and almond cake and cheese souffles and bruschetta and buckwheat blinis and oysters and goat's cheese and poached pears and roasted scallops and pasta with lemon and ham.

This food is so fast it doesn't even need a microwave.

Thirty-eight billion hamburgers are eaten in the United States every year. Imagine if just one-millionth of those were cooked at home, the meat minced with shallot and parsley and a little garlic, the bacon quickly grilled on the spot, the lettuce shredded by the kids, the tomatoes homegrown, the bread warmed, and the wine poured for mum and dad, with the whole family sitting around a table for a meal together. Now, *that*'s fast food.

Fast new food is here to stay. It is politically correct, environmentally friendly, fashionably fashionable and much better for you. Because it is fresh food, cooked very quickly at home, among friends and family.

Fast food is a bed of fresh salad greens instead of a pastry case. It's grilling instead of frying. It's buying the best, freshest produce and doing as little as possible to it.

After all, the less you do to good food, the better. (The same with housework, but that's another story.)

FOOD

silky prawn
wontons
RECIPE 162

new

ENTERTAINING

You're dressed to kill, **or at least maim**. You sweep into the glittering, gilt-ridden restaurant, filled with formal flowers and starched waiters, and glance at the long list of semi-precious Burgundies. Then, an amazing thing happens. You feel it rising in you like a tidal wave. You tense against it, but it overwhelms you. You yawn.

The big night out has lost to *the big night in.*

Good cooking at home will now win friends and influence people every time. After the table-hopping of the 'eighties, we need to relearn the subtlety and complexity of that silent contract between host and guest, and appreciate anew the **delicate nuances** of responsibility that envelop everyone present at the table.

It means taking a risk, which is why even the smallest effort will be appreciated tenfold. And while it means giving more of yourself, it means **paying less**.

Because now that we are entertaining the idea of entertaining at home again, we find that the rules have changed. While it is still a nice ritual to polish the wine glasses and to bring out the best china, we are all **just as happy** with chunky kitchen glasses. And we're likely to be using the best china every night of the week. If it's too good for us, who on earth is it being saved for?

Luckily, this move coincides with a return to **get-real cooking**. No more carrot roses, fancy squiggles in the sauce, or architecturally impossible terrines.

Good home cooking is so **rare** in our lives that it has taken on all the allure a three-star French meal used to have. Mashed potato is the **new foie gras**, garlic is the new truffle, and a slice of fabulous cake is the new soufflé.

Our hard-earned restaurant literacy has given us the confidence to **know good food from bad**, to shop with more style, and to cook with more imagination. Now, all we have to do is realise that there will never be a moment in time when the house will look perfect, and our lives will be **cool and calm** enough to be able to say 'come for dinner', but that we have to say it anyway, and do it anyway.

veal with
prosciutto, sage
and bocconcini
RECIPE 151

149

New Italian

parmigiano gelato
grilled wine bread
veal with prosciutto, sage and bocconcini
short black coffee mascarpone

One of the oldest cuisines in the world is now one of the newest, and the fastest. This instant dinner party is made up of dishes that can either be done beforehand or take mere minutes on the spot — but still look as if you've slaved all day.

Start with a chilled scoop of creamy cheese 'ice-cream' with wine-splattered grilled bread. You can make the gelato a day earlier, while the bread takes seconds to prepare.

Then move on to a very fast flash-in-the-pan dish of tender veal topped with melting bocconcini, fresh sage and prosciutto. Five minutes, and you're back at the table.

Finish with a dramatic mascarpone cream dessert that looks just like espresso coffee. Again, this can — in fact, must — be done ahead of time, so that all you have to do is dust it with cocoa powder to serve.

But don't make it look too easy. You don't want people to know how little you did for them, now, do you?

parmigiano **gelato**

A rich and wonderful presentation of cheese as a first course that I found at New York's Le Madri restaurant. It requires very good parmigiano reggiano, not the packet stuff.

¾ cup grated parmigiano
1 cup pure cream
Freshly ground pepper
¼ teaspoon paprika
1 tablespoon balsamic vinegar

combine cheese, cream, pepper and paprika in the top of a double-boiler or in a heatproof bowl set over simmering water.
whisk while cheese is melting.
remove from heat, strain through a fine sieve, and chill overnight.
using a small ice-cream scoop, place one scoop of gelato on each plate.
drizzle with a few drops of balsamic vinegar and serve with grilled wine bread.

SERVES FOUR

grilled **wine bread**

This rustic accessory to your meal can only be as good as your bread and your wine, so use the best around.

4 slices of crusty, country style bread

1 garlic clove, cut in half

Good red wine

Good olive oil

rub bread with cut side of garlic.

splash bread lightly with red wine to form a nice splotchy pattern.

heat grill or barbecue until hot.

brush bread with a touch of olive oil, and grill on both sides.

S E R V E S   F O U R

parmigiano
gelato and
grilled wine
bread

veal **with prosciutto, sage and bocconcini**

It's worth finding a European-style butcher for the finest, whitest, youngest veal for this drop-dead simple and stylish dish.

3 thin veal fillets (cut for schnitzel)

6 fresh bocconcini

10 fresh sage leaves

6 slices of prosciutto

1 tablespoon olive oil

1 tablespoon butter

1 garlic clove, smashed

½ cup white wine

1 punnet red cherry tomatoes

1 punnet yellow pear tomatoes

bash fillets with a meat mallet until thin.

cut into small 5 cm × 8 cm (2 in × 3 in) squares.

slice bocconcini, and place 2 slices on top of each veal piece.

top with sage leaf, and cover with prosciutto, cut to fit.

slide a toothpick through to hold it.

heat oil, butter, garlic and remaining sage leaves in a large, heavy bottomed pan.

when sizzling, add veal, prosciutto side down, and cook for 2 minutes or so.

turn each fillet, add white wine, and allow wine to bubble and create a little sauce.

transfer veal to warm serving plates, add tomatoes to pan juices, and warm through for 1 minute.

discard garlic, and surround veal with tomatoes.

S E R V E S   S I X

short **black coffee mascarpone**

A do-ahead dessert of fresh mascarpone, flavoured with black Sambuca and espresso coffee. Serve in small espresso coffee cups.

4 free range eggs, separated

3 tablespoons sugar

450 grams (1 pound) mascarpone

2 tablespoons cream

3 tablespoons strong black coffee, cooled

1 tablespoon brandy or cognac

2 tablespoons black Sambuca (Opal Nera) or
   crème de cacao

Cocoa powder for dusting

beat egg yolks with sugar, then blend with mascarpone and cream at high speed.
add coffee, brandy and liqueur.
whip egg whites until stiff and peaky.
gently stir and fold them through the mixture.
serve in small coffee cups, dusted with cocoa powder.

short black
coffee
mascarpone

SERVES SIX

New Bistro

chicken with wine and herbs
creamy potato gratin
upside-down apple tart

Bistro fare is back; heartier, more satisfying, and more delicious than ever before. A snack by the fire, then it's straight to the table for a warm and welcoming chicken casserole, rich with onions and red wine, and with plenty of creamy potatoes on the side.

Then there is time to slip off your shoes, pour another glass, and feast on a caramelised apple tart that has a history as rich as its flavour.

So clear the table of any frippery but for sea salt, a pepper grinder and the crustiest bread you can buy, pop the cork on a chilled bottle of beaujolais, pull up a chair, and eat, talk and drink until the wee, small hours at Bistro Chez Moi, the finest bistro of them all.

chicken with
wine and herbs
and creamy
potato gratin

chicken with wine and herbs

A lighter version of the classic French coq au vin, dotted with mushrooms and small, sweet onions, and flavoured with a good pinot noir.

1 large chicken, cut into 8 or 10 pieces

Salt and freshly ground pepper

3 thick slices of kaiserfleisch or rindless bacon

16 small pickling onions

1 cup small button mushrooms

1 tablespoon butter

1 garlic clove, peeled and smashed

2 tablespoons plain flour

2 tablespoons cognac or brandy

2 sprigs of thyme

4 sprigs of parsley

1 sprig of rosemary

1 bottle pinot noir

1 large tomato

2 bay leaves

More thyme and parsley for serving

salt and pepper chicken.

cut bacon into thick matchsticks, peel onions, trim mushrooms, and roughly chop tomato.

melt butter and cook bacon, onions, mushrooms and garlic until softened, then remove and set aside.

add chicken to the same pan, and brown on all sides for about 10 minutes.

sprinkle flour onto pan, and cook for a couple of minutes, allowing flour to brown.

add cognac and shake pan, taking care if the pan flames momentarily.

return bacon, onions, mushrooms and garlic to the pan.

tie thyme, parsley and rosemary together with string, and add to pan.

add tomato, wine, bay leaves, salt and pepper and bring to the boil.

reduce heat to simmer gently for at least 1 hour, stirring occasionally.

remove garlic and bouquet garni if you can find them, and serve chicken in shallow pasta bowls, dotted with sprigs of fresh thyme or parsley.

SERVES FOUR

creamy potato gratin

An irresistible accompaniment that is always devoured the instant it hits the table.

1 garlic clove, peeled

1 kilo (2 pounds) red-skinned potatoes

2 tablespoons grated gruyère

½ cup crème fraîche or pure cream

1 cup milk

rub a shallow, oval baking dish with garlic.

slice potatoes as thinly as humanly possible.

mix cream and milk.

layer potatoes in the dish, sprinkling with half the cheese and half the milk.

top with remaining cheese, milk and a good pinch of salt.

bake, uncovered, at 180°C (350°F) for 1 hour, until potatoes are cooked and top is crisp and golden.

SERVES FOUR TO SIX

upside-down **apple tart**

They say this famous apple tart was invented in France many years ago by the Tatin sisters, when one of their classic apple tarts fell and broke. So don't worry if yours has a certain rustic charm.

8 golden delicious apples

2 tablespoons butter

¾ cup brown sugar

1 quantity shortcrust pastry (see New Basics page 219)

Cream or crème fraîche for serving

peel, halve and core apples.

melt half the butter in a 20 cm (8 in) baking dish, sprinkle with half the sugar, and arrange apples, cored side up, in concentric circles on top.

pack them in, as they will shrink like crazy during cooking.

top with remaining butter and sugar and cook over medium heat, letting it hiss and bubble like a witches' cauldron for around 30 minutes, until golden brown.

cool in pan.

roll out dough, place over dish and trim so that it falls inside.

bake in a preheated 200°C (400°F) oven for around 30 minutes until pastry is crisp.

now for the scary part.

place a large flat serving dish over the pan and carefully invert.

serve warm from the oven, with a jug of cream or crème fraîche.

SERVES EIGHT

New Moroccan

prawns with chermoula and spicy eggplant

roasted poussin with fruity couscous

oranges and lemons cake

The flavours of Morocco read like an Arabian nights fantasy: almonds, pine nuts, walnuts, pomegranates, yoghurt, lemon-drenched pigeon, salads of oranges and onions, spiced, chargrilled lamb, aromatic stews, paper-thin pastries stuffed with nuts and bathed in syrup, heady with the scents of rose and orange blossom water; a thousand-and-one perfumed, sensual, seductive tastes.

So let us throw our own *diffa* (Moroccan banquet), a golden meal of modern couscous and ancient culture. Start with tangy prawns marinated in chermoula, a traditional marinade for fish and shellfish. Then the main event: a golden, roasted bird on a pile of couscous studded with swollen fruit and nuts.

As for dessert, bake Claudia Roden's fragrant orange and almond cake or just peel fresh white peaches and dust with icing sugar and cinnamon to serve with sweet mint tea.

In the immortal words of Bob Hope and Bing Crosby, 'like Webster's Dictionary, we're Morocco bound'.

prawns **with chermoula and spicy eggplant**

A flashy, colourful dish of tangy, marinated prawns served with a smoky eggplant purée and a spicy red pepper yoghurt sauce.

4 or 5 green (raw) tiger prawns per person

1 teaspoon harissa or chilli paste

1 cup natural yoghurt

Chermoula marinade (see New Basics, page 209)

3 medium eggplants

Olive oil

½ teaspoon cumin

½ teaspoon cinnamon

1 tablespoon lemon juice

Coriander leaves

peel and devein prawns, leaving tail.

stir harissa into yoghurt and chill.

marinate prawns in chermoula marinade for a few hours.

place eggplants on baking tray, drizzle with olive oil, and bake in 200°C (400°F) oven for 40 minutes until skin darkens and blisters.

cool and peel, place flesh in food processor with spices and lemon juice, and blend.

heat a frypan and quickly fry prawns on both sides until flesh just changes colour and they are still glassy in centre.

spoon eggplant purée in centre of each plate, and push prawns into it, sitting up with their tails in the air.

drizzle plate with harissa yoghurt and scatter with picked coriander leaves.

SERVES FOUR

roasted **poussin with fruity couscous**

Golden lemony chicken served on a fruity bed of couscous. To make it even more exotic, serve small bowls of couscous broth (see New Parties, page 195) to one side.

2 tablespoons currants

2 tablespoons sultanas

2 tablespoons dried apricots

1 lemon

4 poussins (spatchcocks or baby chickens)

450 grams (1 pound) couscous (semolina)

1 cup boiling water

1 tablespoon butter

soak dried fruits in water overnight.

cut lemon into quarters, and squeeze the juice of each over each poussin, before tucking it into cavity.

roast poussin in a 180°C (350°F) oven for 30 minutes or until cooked, when juices will run clear.

place couscous in a lightly oiled oven-proof dish, and add water and butter.

stir through, and leave for 5 minutes while couscous absorbs water.

break up any lumps with a fork, mix in drained, soaked fruits, and a little of their water, and heat, covered, at 150°C (300°F) for 20 minutes, tossing occasionally.

spoon couscous and fruits onto warmed plates, and top with roasted poussin.

SERVES FOUR

oranges **and lemons cake**

This cake started off life as a Sephardic orange and almond cake in Claudia Roden's excellent New Book of Middle Eastern Food, *and has been around the world and back since. Here, it has the extra tang of lemons.*

2 oranges

2 lemons

6 free range eggs

1 cup sugar

1 cup ground almonds

1 teaspoon baking powder

place clean, whole and unpeeled fruit in water to cover, and bring to boil.

simmer for 1 hour, until soft.

drain, halve, discard pips and whizz in food processor.

beat eggs and sugar together and add fruit, almonds, and baking powder.

pour into a lightly oiled ring tin or 18 cm (7 in) springform cake tin and bake at 180°C (350°F) for 1 hour, or until top feels firm to the touch.

cool in tin.

leave unadorned or dust with icing sugar to serve.

SERVES SIX

New Indian

crisp-skinned atlantic salmon with indian spices

spicy red lentils

hot date pudding with cardamom toffee sauce

You don't need to cover the table with steaming breads, hot curries, crisp pastries and fragrant rice to spell the magic of India. Just combine a handful of spices with an eye for style and subtlety, and you'll have the flavours of India in a flash.

This highly enjoyable meal starts with a healthy-sized cross-cut of salmon fillet, its skin rubbed with Indian spices and seared until crisp. Serve it on a bed of spiced lentils with a dollop of your favourite chutney. The lentils can be done beforehand, while the salmon cooks on the spot in a minute or two.

Feel free to put out small bowls of natural yoghurt spiked up with ground, roasted cumin seeds, a touch of cayenne pepper and fresh mint leaves. A jar of Indian pickled limes will cause a sensation at the table and in the mouth.

A meal such as this requires only fresh mangoes to finish, or a sticky toffee pudding that will recreate the days of the British Raj.

crisp-skinned **atlantic salmon with indian spices**

The flavours and aromas of your spices will be incomparably better if you buy the whole seed, roast it quickly in a hot, dry pan, and grind it yourself in an electric coffee grinder set aside for your spices.

1 teaspoon ground cumin

1 teaspoon ground coriander seed

½ teaspoon salt

1 teaspoon fennel seeds

1 dessertspoon olive oil

4 thick, wide fillets of Atlantic salmon or ocean trout, with skin

1 tablespoon olive oil

run your fingers gently over fillets to feel where the bones lie, and tweezer them out.

mix spices, moisten skin with a little olive oil, and rub spices into skin.

heat your heaviest bottomed frypan over high heat, and add a very light slick of oil.

when it starts to smoke, add the fish skin side down and cook for a few minutes, moving pan to ensure skin doesn't stick.

turn fish and cook other side for the last few seconds. The skin should be crisp and the flesh still translucently pink.

serve on spicy red lentils, or on mashed potato flavoured with cumin.

SERVES FOUR

spicy **red lentils**

These subtly spiced lentils are the mashed potato of India — the ideal partner for roast chicken, quickly grilled sea scallops and fish.

1 cup red split lentils

4 cups water

½ teaspoon turmeric

½ teaspoon salt

2 tablespoons vegetable or light olive oil

½ teaspoon whole cumin seeds

1 garlic clove, peeled and smashed

1 small onion, peeled and sliced

½ teaspoon coriander seeds

½ teaspoon ground cumin

½ teaspoon cayenne pepper

wash lentils in 3 changes of water, and discard any dark ones.

cook drained lentils in water with salt and turmeric for 30 minutes until soft but not mushy.

drain, and reserve water.

heat oil in heavy bottomed frypan.

when hot, add cumin seeds and fry for 1 minute.

add garlic and onion and fry until golden brown.

add coriander, ground cumin, cayenne and lentils, discard garlic, and cook over low heat for 5 minutes, adding more lentil water if lentils dry out.

SERVES FOUR

hot date pudding with cardamom toffee sauce

Okay, I admit it. There is absolutely nothing Indian about this dish, except for the fact that it is the perfect way to finish this meal.

180 grams (6 ounces) dates, pitted and chopped

1 teaspoon bicarbonate of soda

1 cup boiling water

2 tablespoons butter

180 grams (6 ounces) castor sugar

2 free range eggs

180 grams (6 ounces) self-raising flour

½ teaspoon vanilla essence

Cardamom toffee sauce

140 grams (5 ounces) brown sugar

½ cup cream

1 vanilla bean, split

2 tablespoons butter

4 cardamom pods, crushed

mix dates and bicarbonate of soda.

pour water over dates and leave to stand.

cream butter and sugar until pale.

beat in eggs one at a time.

gently fold in flour, stir in date mixture and vanilla, and pour into a well buttered 18 cm (7 in) square cake tin.

bake at 180°C (350°F) for 30 to 40 minutes, until cooked.

bring sauce ingredients to the boil and simmer for 5 minutes.

cut pudding into squares and place on warm dinner plates.

discard vanilla bean and cardamom pods, pour sauce over pudding and serve.

160 SERVES SIX

New Chinese

silky prawn wontons

eight treasure duck

coconut jelly with star anise fruits

Chinese food is no longer take-away, but stay-home in style. All you need to do is shop well and chop well, and your cooking will be fast and easy.

Start with small but delicious prawn dumplings that can be made ahead of time and simply dropped into a pot of chicken stock to cook for a few minutes before serving.

A magnificent roasted duck, stuffed with edible treasures, can also be prepared beforehand, needing only the final roasting before serving.

Finish with one of my all-time favourite yum cha desserts, the cool and refreshing yai tsup goh, or coconut jelly.

Serve fragrant Chinese tea and aromatic wine, place bowls of crisp nashi pears or fresh lychees on the table, and remember that ancient Chinese proverb 'it is better to eat in than take-away'.

coconut jelly
with star anise
fruits
RECIPE 163

silky prawn wontons

These very sophisticated dumplings are filled with a light prawn mousse for a delicious start to a dinner party.

8 green (raw) prawns, peeled and deveined

1 tablespoon minced pork

1 tablespoon water chestnuts

2 spring onions, finely chopped

1 teaspoon dry sherry

Salt and pepper

1 egg white

Large wonton wrappers

1 teaspoon cornflour mixed with 1 tablespoon cold water

2 cups chicken stock or water for poaching

place prawns, pork, water chestnuts, spring onions, sherry, salt and pepper in food processor and mix to a paste.

remove to a bowl, and beat in the egg white until mixture stiffens.

place a teaspoonful of mixture in centre of each wonton wrapper.

dip finger in cornflour water and run it along each of the 4 edges.

bring all 4 corners up to a point in the middle, and press along each edge to seal.

poach for 3 or 4 minutes in simmering chicken stock or water. Drain and serve.

SERVES SIX

eight treasure duck

A glorious golden roasted duck, cut open at the table to reveal chestnuts, rice and pork. Order the duck tunnel-boned from the tail end with wing bones removed but drumsticks intact.

1 cup glutinous or short grain rice, soaked in cold water for 2 hours

4 dried Chinese mushrooms

20 dried Chinese shrimps

1 size 16 duck, tunnel-boned

2 tablespoons peanut oil

200 grams (7 ounces) minced pork or chicken

1 tablespoon Chinese rice wine or dry sherry

2 tablespoons soy sauce

2 tablespoons water chestnuts, coarsely chopped

2 tablespoons Chinese roast pork (char sieu), finely diced

400 gram (14 ounce) can of whole chestnuts in water

Salt to taste

line steamer with greaseproof paper and steam drained rice for 20 minutes.

soak mushrooms and shrimps in water for 30 minutes.

drain mushrooms, discard stems and slice finely.

remove any loose fat from duck, and rub with salt.

heat wok or frypan, and add oil.

when hot, add minced pork or chicken and stir fry for a few minutes until brown.

add wine and soy sauce, stirring, then mushrooms, chopped water chestnuts, rice, roast pork, and drained shrimps, and toss to mix thoroughly, cooking for a few minutes more.

remove from heat, gently mix in the whole chestnuts and their water, and cool.

heat oven to 220°C (425°F) and prepare trussing needle and string.

sew up the neck opening, stuff the duck loosely then sew up the tail opening.

mould the body into a vaguely duck-like shape.

place breast-side up on a lightly oiled rack set over a roasting tin half-filled with water.

bake for 30 minutes.

reduce heat to 180°C (350°F) for 1 hour.

gently remove string, and carve at the table. By cutting straight across the body, everyone gets a slice of crisp skin, tender meat, and rich stuffing.

SERVES SIX

coconut **jelly with star anise fruits**

A yum cha favourite known as yai tsup goh is exquisite on its own or dressed up for dinner with fragrant fruits in syrup.

2 cups water

2 tablespoons powdered gelatine

180 grams (6 ounces) sugar

200 millilitres (7 fluid ounces) coconut milk

4 egg whites

2 tablespoons sugar

2 star anise

2 cups water

Lychees, rambutan, grapes, star fruit and berries

boil water, gelatine and sugar and stir until dissolved.

add coconut milk, and leave to cool for 1 or 2 hours, stirring once or twice.

whisk egg whites until stiff and fluffy, and whisk into cooled coconut milk.

pour into a wet rectangular 15 cm (6 in) square cake tin and chill for at least 2 hours before cutting into squares and serving.

add sugar and star anise to water and bring to boil, stirring.

peel lychees and rambutan, slice star fruit, and add all fruit to the poaching liquid.

simmer for 5 minutes, and allow to cool in liquid. Drain and serve with coconut jelly.

SERVES FOUR TO SIX

New Med

grilled zucchini with roasted red peppers
grilled fish chop with chickpea pasta
red fruits with yoghurt and honey

The sun-washed flavours of the Mediterranean shine brightly over dull diets everywhere. Crisp vegetables, ripe tomatoes, fresh fish, lean meat, wholesome breads, sun-ripened melons, red wine and energy-giving pulses, grains and pasta bring health and a wealth of colour and good taste.

Roast your red peppers beforehand so that all you have to do on the spot is flash-grill the zucchini strips for a colourful start to the meal.

For the main course, you can cook the chickpeas and pasta and marinate the fish chops beforehand.

The brilliantly coloured fruits and their ambrosial yoghurt and honey sauce can both be done hours earlier.

With such easy, breezy food, a formal dinner table would seem out of place. Keep the mood sunny and casual, and pile fruits and flowers high in pyramids of freshness.

Then all you need do is propose a toast to the Mediterranean and to the relaxed nature of its meals, and enjoy yourself.

grilled fish chop with chickpea pasta
RECIPE 166

grilled **zucchini with roasted red peppers**

The spirit and brilliant colours of the Mediterranean, with all the nutritional value you need to get you through the 'nineties.

3 red capsicums
2 tablespoons olive oil
Salt and freshly ground pepper
1 tablespoon capers
4 zucchini
1 tablespoon small black olives

bake capsicums at 180°C (350°F) for 30 minutes, or until skin blisters and starts to blacken.

remove and place in a covered bowl for 10 minutes.

core, deseed, and peel.

cut flesh into thin strips, and toss with 1 tablespoon of oil, salt, pepper and capers.

slice zucchini very thinly lengthwise, baste with remaining oil and grill for 6 to 8 minutes, turning once.

arrange zucchini around the capsicum, scatter black olives on top and serve.

SERVES FOUR

grilled **fish chop with chickpea pasta**

Fish tastes best when cooked on the bone (but not overcooked). Here, chunky deep sea cutlets are flavoured with chermoula, a Moroccan marinade of fresh herbs, spices and lemon juice.

6 cutlets of fresh fish (trevalla, tuna, schnapper or salmon)

Chermoula marinade (see New Basics, page 209)

1 cup dried chickpeas, soaked overnight

1 cup small dried pasta

1 red capsicum

3 zucchini

3 plum tomatoes

1 tablespoon olive oil

3 sprigs of fresh thyme

Salt and freshly ground pepper

1 tablespoon basil leaves

1 tablespoon fresh parsley, chopped

marinate fish in chermoula for 3 hours.

cook chickpeas in simmering salted water for 1 hour or until tender.

cook pasta in simmering, salted water for 10 minutes.

core and deseed capsicum and cut into small squares.

cut zucchini and tomatoes into small dice.

add olive oil and thyme to a large pan, and gently heat to infuse oil.

add vegetables and cook until soft.

add chickpeas, pasta, salt, pepper and herbs, and heat.

grill fish, drizzle with remaining marinade and serve with chickpea pasta.

SERVES SIX

red **fruits with yoghurt and honey**

Sweet, sun-ripened fresh fruit gains a healthy blush from rose petal syrup and berry liqueur.

Fresh red fruits in season: melons, peaches, plums, berries

1 cup fresh mint leaves

½ cup strawberry liqueur

½ cup rose petal syrup

Dry white wine

1 cup natural yoghurt

1 tablespoon honey

½ teaspoon vanilla essence

prepare fruit as you see fit, and gently combine with mint leaves in a large bowl.

add liqueur, syrup, and white wine to almost cover, and chill for several hours.

blend yoghurt, honey and vanilla in food processor, and serve in a separate bowl.

SERVES FOUR

New Thai

white noodle salad
whole fish with ham, chilli and ginger
grilled lemon grass fruits

Thai food must be the brightest, boldest, happiest, tangiest food in the world. Almost every meal combines the bite of chilli, the tang of fresh lemon grass, the sourness of tamarind, the blanketing creaminess of coconut milk and the fragrance of jasmine rice. No wonder everyone in Thailand smiles all the time.

This meal starts with a tangy white noodle salad, drenched in lime juice and crunchy with peanuts, which can be made before your guests arrive.

The whole fish is cooked on the spot, although you can prepare all ingredients beforehand and have them in bowls, ready to go.

As for the skewers of fresh fruit, you can choose whether to serve the fruit raw, simply sprinkled with sugar, salt and chilli, or grill them and serve warm and slightly caramelised.

white **noodle salad**

The delicate texture of these transparent noodles, available from all Asian food stores, is the highlight of this refreshing yum woon sen adapted from Charmaine Solomon's Thai Cookbook.

2 cups bean starch noodles

1 teaspoon peanut oil

1 cup fresh shrimps

1 garlic clove, crushed

2 tablespoons salted beer nuts, chopped

2 tablespoons fish sauce (nam pla)

2 tablespoons spring onions, finely chopped

2 tablespoons coriander, finely chopped

Juice of 2 limes

2 red chillies, finely chopped

2 tablespoons dried shrimps, ground to a powder

drop noodles into a pot of boiling water for 3 or 4 minutes until they lose their crunch.
drain, rinse, and reserve.
heat oil and fry shrimps quickly.
toss shrimps with all the other ingredients in a large bowl, and serve at room temperature.

SERVES FOUR

whole fish with ham, chilli and ginger

A remarkably easy main course, as long as you succeed in turning the fish in the wok without losing its tail or your temper.

1 whole fleshy fish (schnapper, bream, nannygai), clean and dry

5 cm (2 in) knob of fresh ginger, peeled

2 slices of ham

1 green capsicum

1 red capsicum

2 spring onions

1 cup water

½ teaspoon sugar

3 tablespoons fish sauce (nam pla)

1 teaspoon roughly ground pepper

8 tablespoons peanut oil

3 garlic cloves, smashed

3 small red chillies, sliced

Fresh coriander, chopped

cut 3 slashes into the thickest part of fish on both sides, and snip off fins.

cut ginger, ham, capsicums and spring onions into thin matchstick lengths.

combine water, sugar, fish sauce and pepper in a bowl and reserve.

heat oil in wok, and carefully slide in fish.

move wok around as fish cooks.

turn fish after 5 or 6 minutes, taking care not to break tail.

when cooked, remove fish to 2 warm plates.

remove all but 1 or 2 tablespoons of oil from the wok, then add ginger and garlic and cook, stirring for 1 minute.

add ham, capsicums and chillies and cook for 2 minutes.

add combined sauce ingredients, and bubble for 30 seconds to thicken slightly.

pour sauce over fish, sprinkle with coriander, and serve with jasmine rice.

S E R V E S   F O U R

grilled lemon grass fruits

Nothing beats fresh fruit after the sweet heat of a Thai meal. These fresh fruits are heaven on a stick eaten fresh, or grilled.

3 lemon grass stalks, white part only

4 wooden satay skewers

Mango, banana, pawpaw, pineapple, lychees, star fruit, grapes, or berries

Juice of 1 lime

4 teaspoons sugar

½ teaspoon salt

1 red chilli, seeded and finely chopped

1 lime

bash lemon grass stems until bruised, and cut into matchstick lengths.

soak skewers and lemon grass in water for a few hours, so they will not burn.

cut fruit into pieces and arrange on skewers, divided by lengths of lemon grass.

squeeze lime juice and sprinkle sugar, salt and a little chilli on each skewer.

grill until sugar bubbles and caramelises.

slip a segment of fresh lime on the end of each skewer, and serve.

S E R V E S   F O U R

white noodle salad

RECIPE 167

P A S

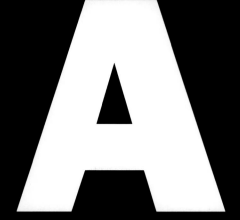

There is nothing nicer than soft, fresh pasta, cooked in seconds and topped with a spoonful of pesto, a splodge of ripe tomato infused in olive oil and basil, or just a touch of butter and grated parmigiano reggiano.

Fresh pasta is very seductive, and very flexible. You can fill it with ricotta cheese, prawns, fish, spinach or meat. You can buy sheets of it, and cut out your own shapes. You can cut it into squares and build your own lasagna on each serving plate, separating the sheets with warm goat's cheese, roasted red capsicum, and grilled eggplant.

You can serve it as noodles in your favourite soup, or next to a little quickly cooked veal, or under marinated and grilled chicken.

It is well worth investing in your future happiness by buying a small hand-turned pasta machine.

Making pasta is therapeutic, soothing, and very, very rewarding. You will need two cups of plain flour, two large fresh eggs, one tablespoon of olive oil, two teaspoons of lukewarm water, a pinch of salt, a little time and a fine opera resounding through the house.

first, pile flour into a mound on your work bench and make a hole in the centre. Break eggs into the hole, and add olive oil, water and salt.

beat this egg mixture with a fork or with your fingers, then continue to beat, slowly drawing in a little of the flour each time.

when half the flour has been incorporated, use the palms of your hands to knead the dough, pushing away from you, and gathering in more flour as you go.

when most of the flour is incorporated, scrape the bench clean, and lightly flour the bench and your hands.

knead the dough for five or ten minutes. That master of pasta Guiliano Bugialli of Florence, who leaves flour from one end of the kitchen to the other when making pasta and talking at the same time, says to continue kneading until you can stick your finger in the centre and it comes out dry. If it is sticky, keep kneading, adding more flour.

next, set the rollers of your pasta machine at their widest point (number one).

cut a small section of pasta from the dough, flatten it, dust it with flour, and feed it through the machine. Repeat this four or five times.

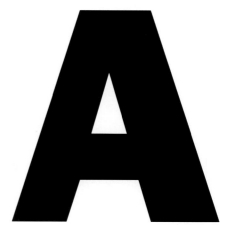

then change the notch of the pasta machine to the next setting, and feed the pasta through once. **continue** through successively smaller settings until you reach your desired thickness.

Now, you have options. You can cut the pasta into tagliatelle on the machine, cut it by hand into wide strips of pappardelle, gently rub it through a harp-like chitarra, or turn it into cannelloni, tortelloni, ravioli, or lasagna.

You can hang the pasta to dry on a wooden rack or floured broom handle, arrange it in soft bundles to dry, freeze it, or store it on an uncovered tray in a cool place for up to one month.

Fine, fresh pasta needs very little cooking. Just drop it into a big pot of salted, boiling water for a minute or two.

Then there is dried pasta, a magnificent product made of high protein durum wheat flour.

Normal supermarket pasta is like normal supermarket white sliced bread, with little flavour or texture. Look a little further, and you will find pasta with character, breeding and intelligence.

Try Martelli spaghetti and spaghettini, bred in a castle in Lari, near Pisa, and kneaded twice as long as other dried pastas. Unlike most commercial varieties which are extruded through Teflon dies, the Martelli company still uses the older, more expensive bronze dies to give a truer shape and form. A solid, substantial pasta, it will bring class to the lowliest occasion, although it is at its best on Sunday nights tossed with a crunchy shower of grilled bacon and a whole egg broken into it and stirred through while still piping hot.

Or go for broke with Cipriani tagliolini, a pasta so insinuating, so luxurious, and so decadent, nobody can remain untouched by its presence. It is fine, frail, and feminine, and needs only a couple of minutes cooking in plenty of rolling, boiling water. It is at its best with a sauce of grated lemon rind, white wine and cream, but I love it with roasted blue eye cod tossed in olive oil and toasted breadcrumbs, or with a spoonful of rich walnut sauce.

As for the old question about whether fresh or dried pasta is best, there can only be one answer. Both.

new PICNICS

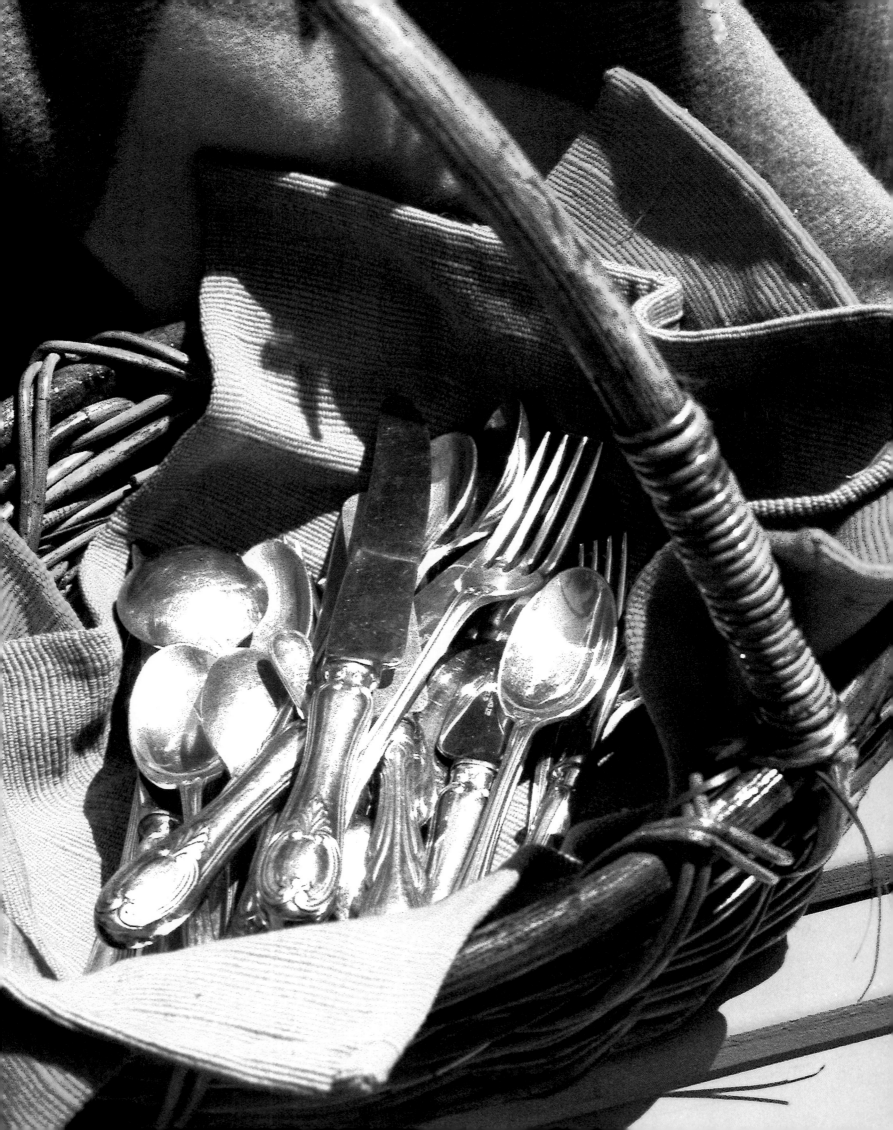

Picnics were invented long before recessions, door buster sales, dysfunctional families or oil-free mayonnaise. Yet they attain a certain piquancy, **an extra relish**, during tough times. It's good to sit under a cloudless blue sky or an ancient, leafy tree, and know you're not paying for the overheads.

Whatever you do, don't take a simple, wonderful concept like a picnic and make it complicated. **Reduce** a picnic to its **essentials**: all you need is a good ground rug, a vacuum flask for hot, milky coffee or fragrant Chinese tea, lots of paper napkins, great bread — the sort you can turn into a serviceable boat if the kayak overturns — and plenty of *good, strong, easy food.*

You must also have a sense of humour and a good pocket knife, because somebody (probably you) is going to **leave the corkscrew** at home.

The food is actually the easy part. After all, everything tastes wonderful when served with **fresh air** and a beautiful view. These days, it is finding the perfect picnic spot that is difficult.

Just when you've settled into your leafy sylvan setting twenty kilometres from the nearest gym, along comes a gust of wind and a black cloud. Or a battalion of gourmet ants, closely followed by a squadron of flies. Or a rat-tat-tat trail bike.

No wonder the latest trend in outdoor eating is **to eat indoors**. One of my favourite picnics was served on a checked rug in front of a roaring log fire on the living room floor of a friend, while the rain turned the windows grey and the wind howled at the door. It was wonderful!

So pack a perfect picnic, and **venture out** — or in.

Take **Greek dips** to be scooped up with pita bread, marinated and grilled chicken wings, crumbed veal or chicken schnitzels, meatballs, old-fashioned **egg-and-bacon pie** with whole eggs in it, cold meats and pickles, pork pies and terrines, cold roast chicken, and bunches of grapes, and head off into the wide blue yonder. Or into the living room.

provençal salad
in a roll
RECIPE 176

provençal **salad in a roll**

This refreshing salad inside bread is the perfect low-maintenance picnic fare.

2 long, crusty French breadsticks (baguette or ficelle)

2 tablespoons red wine vinegar

1 garlic clove, crushed

1 teaspoon Dijon mustard

Salt and freshly ground pepper

4 tablespoons virgin olive oil

Handful of mixed salad greens

200 gram (7 ounce) canned tuna

4 anchovy fillets, drained and rinsed

2 eggs, hard-boiled, peeled and sliced

1 tablespoon tiny capers, drained

12 black olives, stoned

1 red capsicum, finely sliced

1 onion, peeled and finely sliced

3 ripe red tomatoes, finely sliced

cut breadsticks into 4 equal lengths, then halve and scoop out some of the bread.

mix vinegar, garlic, mustard, salt and pepper, and whisk in olive oil to make dressing.

toss a few mixed salad leaves in dressing and remove, then moisten scooped out bread in dressing.

build each roll, starting with leaves, adding tuna, anchovies, egg, capers, olives, capsicum, onion, tomatoes, and soaked bread.

top with other half of roll, and tie tightly with string.

wrap in plastic and chill for 2 hours before taking on picnic.

176   SERVES FOUR

hummus **and tomato salad**

Use pita or pocket bread to scoop up the tangy, fresh hummus, topped with a light, bright tomato salad.

2 cups chickpeas, soaked in water overnight

3 tablespoons lemon juice

3 tablespoons tahini (sesame seed paste)

2 garlic cloves, crushed

½ teaspoon ground cumin

2 tablespoons olive oil

Salt and freshly ground pepper

3 ripe tomatoes

1 cucumber

1 tablespoon extra virgin olive oil

½ tablespoon red wine vinegar

6 rounds pocket bread, Turkish flat bread or pita bread

cover soaked and drained chickpeas in cold water and cook until tender.

purée in food processor with lemon juice, tahini, garlic, cumin, olive oil, salt and pepper.

stop and taste, adding more garlic, lemon juice or cumin as desired.

chop tomatoes into small dice.

peel cucumber, cut in half, scoop out seeds, and cut into small dice.

mix with tomato, oil, vinegar, salt and pepper, and spoon on top of hummus in a shallow bowl.

serve with lots of bread for dipping.

SERVES SIX

hummus and
tomato salad

chilli fetta cheese

A simple marinated fetta cheese dish that will freshen up any picnic, brunch or lunch.

1 cup good fetta cheese

1 fresh red chilli, sliced

2 tablespoons small black olives

2 tablespoons extra virgin olive oil

1 tablespoon small capers

Freshly ground pepper

Fresh rosemary or dried oregano

mix chilli, olives, olive oil, capers, pepper and herb, and pour over fetta cheese.

cover and leave overnight.

cut into small bricks and serve with bread, drizzled with the marinade.

SERVES FOUR TO SIX

lemon leaf meatballs

Lemon leaves give these popular meatballs a freshness and flavour that is hard to resist. Serve with a lemon and yoghurt dipping sauce (see New Basics, page 211).

2 cups day old bread, torn

1 cup milk

450 grams (1 pound) minced veal, chicken or both

½ cup grated parmigiano

Salt and freshly ground pepper

2 garlic cloves, crushed

2 tablespoons parsley, finely chopped

Juice of 1 lemon

Grated rind of 1 lemon

20 lemon leaves

soak bamboo satay sticks in water for 1 hour beforehand.

soak bread in milk for 10 minutes, and squeeze dry.

mix meat, bread, cheese, salt, pepper, garlic, parsley, lemon juice and lemon rind together with your hands. If mixture seems too heavy, add a little of the milk.

roll into balls the size of a walnut.

wash and dry lemon leaves, and wrap each meatball in a leaf.

thread 3 meatballs and leaves on sticks.

grill meat side down until cooked. The leaves will burn, but will give a delicious smoky lemon flavour to the meat.

MAKES TWENTY MEATBALLS

chilli fetta
cheese

roasted **pepper salad**

Whenever you see glorious green and red capsicums, turn them into this salad, grab a packet of crisp grissini and a bottle of wine, and set off on a picnic immediately.

3 red capsicums

3 green capsicums

2 tablespoons olive oil

Salt and freshly ground pepper

1 tablespoon capers

1 tablespoon black olives

rub capsicums with a little of the olive oil and bake at 180°C (350°F) for 30 minutes, or until skin blisters and starts to blacken.

place in a covered bowl for 10 minutes.

core, seed and peel capsicums.

cut flesh into thin strips, and toss with remaining oil, salt, pepper, capers and olives.

SERVES SIX

little egg and
bacon pies

little **egg and bacon pies**

An old Australian favourite, updated into small individual pies.

1 packet of filo pastry

2 tablespoons butter, melted

2 rindless rashers bacon

7 free range eggs

½ cup milk

Salt and freshly ground pepper

1 tablespoon parsley, chopped

½ teaspoon sweet paprika

brush one layer of filo pastry with melted butter.

add another layer and brush.

continue until you have 6 layers.

cut in half, and gently drape pastry inside 2 small pie tins.

repeat process until you have 6 pastry-lined pie tins.

trim edges of pastry roughly.

chop bacon and distribute among pie tins.

beat 1 egg with milk, salt, pepper and parsley, and distribute evenly.

break 1 egg into each pie, and bake in a preheated 200°C (400°F) oven for 10 minutes.

reduce heat to 180°C (350°F) for another 5 to 10 minutes, until egg is set and pastry is crisp and golden.

gently remove from tin and allow to cool before taking on picnic.

MAKES SIX

artichoke **heart, leek and cheese tart**

This warm, cheesy frittata-style pie is easy to make, and easy to eat. It also makes a good supper when the sun goes down, made with whatever is left in the cupboard.

3 small leeks

1 tablespoon butter

1 tablespoon olive oil

6 free range eggs

2 tablespoons grated parmigiano

3 tablespoons milk

Salt and freshly ground pepper

6 artichoke hearts, preserved in oil

cut down into the long green leaves of the leeks, and wash well.

slice into fine rings.

heat butter and oil in frypan, and cook leeks until almost soft.

break eggs into bowl and stir in cheese, milk, salt and pepper.

lower heat under leeks, and pour egg mixture into pan, gently stirring.

drain artichoke hearts and arrange in pan, and cook slowly for 20 minutes.

cook top by sliding frypan under the griller for the last few minutes.

eat warm if you're picnicking nearby, or cool if you're venturing far away.

SERVES FOUR

chicken **salad souvlaki**

Instead of taking chicken, salad and bread, combine all three in one wonderful chicken salad souvlaki that can be rolled up and eaten in the hands.

4 roasted lemon poussin (see page 182)

1 bunch spinach

1 tablespoon lemon juice

1 tablespoon butter

4 ripe red tomatoes

2 tablespoons red wine vinegar

4 rounds of Greek pita bread

1 tablespoon olive oil

1 cup fetta cheese, crumbled

2 tablespoons small black olives, pitted

2 tablespoons fresh mint leaves

1 tablespoon dried oregano

1 cup natural yoghurt

remove breast of chicken and slice. Remove drumsticks and take along as an extra snack.

wash spinach of all grit, and shake dry.

cut tomatoes into wedges and marinate in red wine vinegar for 1 hour.

toss spinach in olive oil, drain and place on bread.

top with sliced chicken, tomato, fetta, olives, mint leaves and oregano.

roll up and tie with raffia to take on picnic.

serve with yoghurt.

MAKES FOUR

lemon-crusted **chicken schnitzels**

A fragrant, crisp crumb crust seals in the tenderness of these chicken schnitzels. Take your favourite chutney or relish to serve with them.

4 chicken fillets

1 cup fine breadcrumbs

Grated rind of 1 lemon

Salt and freshly ground pepper

¼ teaspoon sweet paprika

1 free range egg, lightly beaten

2 tablespoons plain flour

1 tablespoon olive oil

1 tablespoon butter

lay chicken fillets out on board and flatten with a meat mallet or equivalent.

cut each fillet in half.

mix lemon rind, breadcrumbs, salt and pepper and paprika.

dip each fillet in beaten egg, then in flour, and then in flavoured breadcrumbs.

heat oil and butter until foaming, add schnitzels and fry until golden brown and tender.

drain on kitchen paper and allow to cool before taking on picnic.

MAKES EIGHT

roasted **lemon poussin**

If you haven't preserved your lemons in salt and lemon juice yet (see New Basics, page 208), you can use fresh lemons, as long as you don't mind missing out on an incredible flavour difference.

8 poussins (spatchcocks or baby chickens)

Grated rind of 4 lemons

4 garlic cloves, smashed

2 preserved (or fresh) lemons, quartered

Salt and freshly ground pepper

1 tablespoon butter, melted

Juice of 2 lemons

Extra lemons for garnish

clean poussin and wipe dry.

rub grated lemon rind over skin, and slip garlic and a preserved lemon quarter into cavity of each bird.

season with salt and pepper.

roast poussin for 30 to 40 minutes at 180°C (350°F), basting occasionally with melted butter and lemon juice, until juices of thigh run clear when pierced with skewer.

serve piled high on a platter with quarters of fresh lemons.

SERVES EIGHT

couscous **and tomato salad**

A bright and happy salad of light-as-air semolina spiked with parsley, spring onions, cherry tomatoes and coloured capsicums.

450 grams (1 pound) couscous

Salt and freshly ground pepper

2 cups parsley, finely chopped

Juice of 2 lemons

3 tablespoons olive oil

1 punnet red cherry tomatoes

1 punnet yellow pear tomatoes

1 red capsicum

1 yellow capsicum

1 green capsicum

6 spring onions, washed and trimmed

put couscous in large bowl, and pour on 2 · cups of boiling water.

stir through, and leave, covered, for 30 minutes.

using 2 forks, fluff up the couscous and get rid of any lumps.

add parsley, lemon juice and oil, and toss to mix.

halve tomatoes, and chop spring onions finely.

chop capsicum into small cubes, discarding seeds and core.

toss vegetables through couscous, mixing well, and serve.

SERVES SIX

couscous and
tomato salad

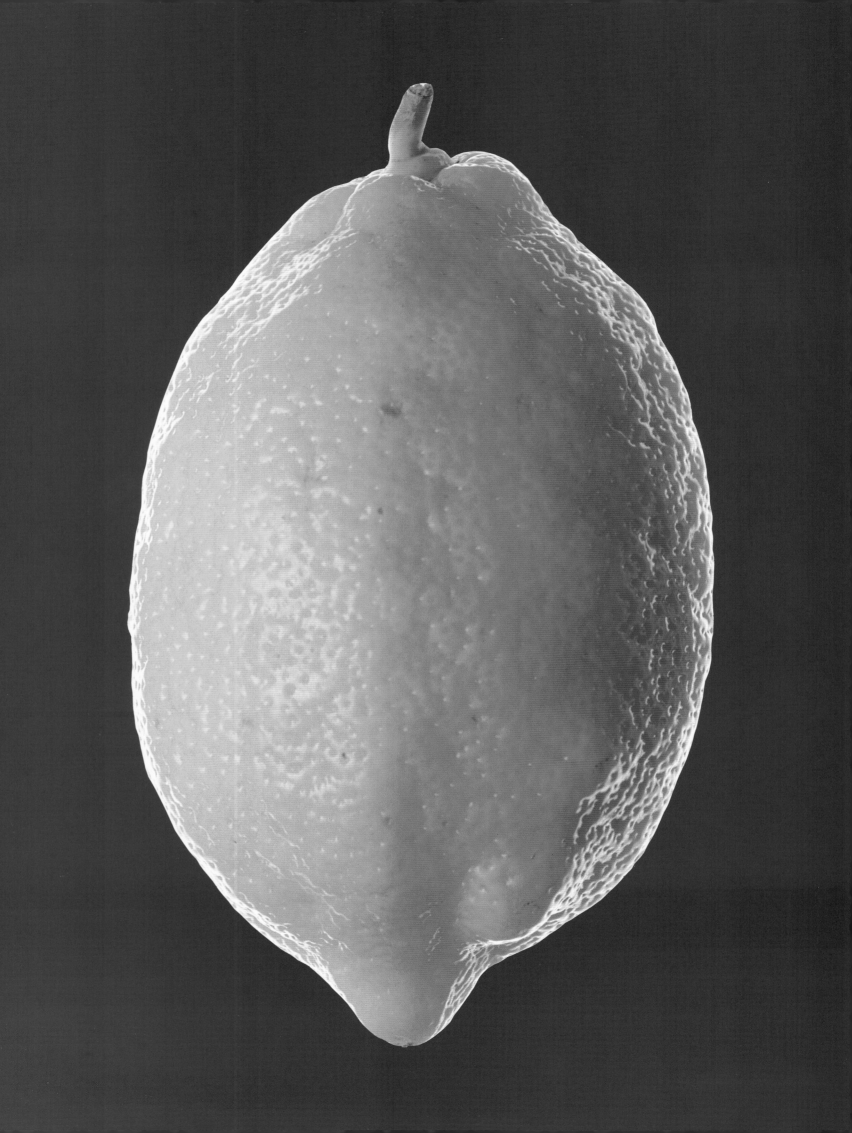

lemons

If there seem to be a lot of lemon flavoured recipes in this book, you're right. The lemon is perfect New Food, because it is easy to get, easy to use, and can transform a dish from nice but dull to bright and breezy in a single squeeze.

The lemon is a refreshingly simple, happy fruit that comes in no-nonsense, house-brand packaging that lends itself to all occasions.

The yellow rind, or flavedo, releases a spray of essential oil when twisted, while pectin from the white pith is used to thicken breakfast marmalades.

The juice is used to pep up vegetables, make summer drinks more cordial, whiten red elbows, and clean the stains from the murky interiors of countless vacuum flasks.

Slipping in slices of lemon when boiling eggs prevents rings from forming in the saucepan.

Half a cut lemon rubbed over your chopping board will eat up the odours of onion, garlic and fish, while the other half will enhance the flavour of the finished dish.

I always save up squeezed lemons to throw into the washing-up water. It may not clean the dishes any faster, but at least I enjoy the smell.

Both India and China claim to be the ancient birthplace of the lemon, although India, according to historians, is the more logical choice. There are now over twenty-one official varieties throughout the world, inciting both sweet and sour national emotions. In Spain, they love the verna lemon, while Italy adores the femminello ovale. Australians like the Lisbon, a native Portuguese, and the fragrant Meyer.

Lemons taste best when left to ripen on the tree. Unfortunately common commercial practice is to pick lemons while still green, because the high acid content helps them last longer in storage. They are then 'de-greened' with a gassing of ethylene oxide, which turns their chlorophyll-green into lemon-yellow.

This trick of picking unripe fruit was first practised by Portuguese seafarers, who discovered the scurvy-preventing Vitamin C qualities of lemons, and went on to discover the world, planting lemon trees in all their regular ports-of-call. (Thanks, guys.)

So squeeze lemon into your risotto, into your poached fruits, and over your chargrilled vegetables. The best pasta sauce in the world starts with lemon rind cooked in a little butter and white wine, touched with cream and cayenne pepper and splashed with lemon juice, grated parmigiano and pepper just before it hits the table.

So give your cooking the golden glow of the lusty lemon, the rude health of the rind, and the passion of the pith. Those other fruits couldn't fight their way out of a paper bag.

n e w PARTIES

tiger prawn
spring rolls
RECIPE 197

Whatever happened to parties?

It seems houses have grown smaller and expenses have grown larger, until the only gatherings of more than ten people these days are at weddings and wakes.

It's time we learnt how to throw **a new sort** of party. Instead of organising everything ourselves, we can organise everyone else to organise everything. Write a list of the sort of things you want, from crisps and candles to cakes and cabernet, then tell everyone **what to bring**. Or get a few friends together and cohost a party, as the school kids do. That way, you can **share the ideas**, the costs, and the cleaning up.

To throw a new party, you need both style and a smile. When in doubt, go for a theme, because it makes all other decisions easy, and gives you simple ideas for food, drink and decor. And **never overestimate** the maturity and intelligence of your friends. What works at little kids' parties will work for the big kids, too.

You have to be generous with your food, your wine, your grace and your charm, and extremely selfish in choosing who to invite and what to eat.

You have an obligation to serve the **best wine** you can afford, and enough delicious food to soak up the alcohol. The food must be in a form that can be eaten without looking like an idiot, and should preferably come in **industrial-sized portions**.

Get a whole wheel of brie or a huge wedge of parmigiano instead of a supermarket selection of sad-wrapped little cheese slices. Fill baskets with bread, laundry tubs with ice, and have **ten times as many glasses** as you need, because you will need them all, unless you want to spend all your time at the sink.

And do one thing, just one, that will shake people out of their normal party politeness, and **leave them feeling spoilt**, surprised and happy. It could be the food, the champagne, the music, a special guest, a special theme, or a 'happening' of some kind. After all, you want them to remember you fondly, or they may not invite you to *their* party. And then we'd be back where we started, without any party at all.

pandan chicken
RECIPE 198

The antipasto party

Don't tell the Italians, but they have been getting it wrong for many, many years. The Italian word 'antipasto' literally means before the meal, and has come to mean that colourful explosion of glistening vegetables, rich, red meats, golden cheeses and juicy olives eaten before the main course.

But a good antipasto is a meal in itself. The unctuous oiliness of one dish leads you on to the snappy crunch of another, and onward, ever onward through the sweet, the sour, the rich, the lean, the modern and the ancient.

There will be bowls of olives, of course, and sun-dried tomatoes, grissini, pyramids of fresh fruit and trays of freshly sliced prosciutto, pancetta and salami. Try threading cubes of melon on wooden skewers, interlaced with pale pink ribbons of prosciutto, or wrapping fresh ripe figs in prosciutto.

To finish, just cut into an icy cold watermelon, or serve grapes and cherries in big glass bowls of iced water spiked with fresh mint. A few Italian amaretti biscuits wouldn't go astray with espresso coffee and a glass of Strega, Sambuca or Amaretto.

veal and chicken polpettini

Moist, fragrant meatballs of veal and chicken from party pal Dolly Campbell. Double the recipe and make sixty. There is no limit to what people eat when they're having a good time.

2 cups torn dry bread

1 cup milk

250 grams (9 ounces) minced veal

250 grams (9 ounces) minced chicken

½ cup grated parmigiano

Salt and freshly ground pepper

2 garlic cloves, crushed

2 tablespoons finely chopped parsley

Grated rind of 1 lemon

Flour for dusting

3 tablespoons olive oil

Juice of 1 lemon

soak bread in milk, and squeeze dry.

mix bread with meats, cheese, salt, pepper, garlic, parsley and lemon rind, using your hands.

add a little of the milk if the mixture seems too heavy.

roll into small balls between your palms, and dust lightly with flour.

heat oil in a heavy based frypan, and cook meatballs until golden brown, turning them to brown evenly.

drain on paper towel and sprinkle with a little lemon juice.

serve warm or cold, with a spicy grilled tomato sauce (see New Basics, page 217).

MAKES THIRTY

veal and chicken polpettini

tomato **and basil bruschetta**

A great mopper-upper of too much wonderful wine, and even better topped with olive tapenade (see New Basics, page 208).

4 garlic cloves
1 cup extra virgin olive oil
10 ripe tomatoes
Salt and freshly ground pepper
1 cup fresh basil leaves
2 loaves of crusty country style bread

smash garlic and add to olive oil.

slice tomatoes, sprinkle with salt and pepper, and add to olive oil.

tear basil leaves and add, then leave to mingle for a few hours.

heat grill, and grill bread.

brush quickly with garlicky olive oil.

top with slices of tomato and basil, and serve to the hordes.

SERVES TEN

———

tomato and
basil bruschetta

———

The pizza party

If your friends are the sort you wouldn't trust with your best glasses — and let's face it, most of our best friends are that sort — then go casual, and get away with maximum hospitality and minimum household damage.

Stock up on stacks of cheap glasses, and turn the kitchen into a late-night pizza parlour.

These are the sort of pizze you can't get at the end of a telephone — crisp, biscuity bases topped with sheer quality ingredients.

Necessities include fresh bocconcini, good quality salami, prosciutto, pancetta, tomato paste or passato, herbs like fresh basil, thyme and oregano, anchovies, olives, and roasted peppers.

As well, there are wonderful things you can cook up beforehand to add variety, like sweet onion marmalade, grilled tomato sauce, pesto and olive tapenade, all found in New Basics.

Lay everything out on big platters, precook your pizza bases and invite everyone to make their own tailor-made pizza. Then again, knowing your friends, it might be better to have a designated cook who takes orders, cooks, and stays off the red wine.

———

goat's cheese
and spinach
pizza
RECIPE 194

———

goat's **cheese and spinach pizza**

A bright and lively combination of lemony goat's milk cheese and fresh, good-for-you spinach that will keep the party going long after it should have faded away.

Bunch of spinach

2 pizza bases (see New Basics, page 212)

2 tablespoons tomato passato

12 thin slices of fresh goat's cheese

12 or more small black olives

12 sun-dried tomatoes

Oil from sun-dried tomato jar

heat oven to 200°C (400°F).

cut stems from spinach, and clean spinach carefully under cold running water.

toss into a pot of simmering water for 30 seconds until limp, then drain, cool and squeeze dry.

brush 2 pizza bases with tomato passato.

top with well drained spinach, scattered roughly.

add thin slices of goat's cheese, a few small black olives and a few sliced sun dried tomatoes.

drizzle with the oil from the sun-dried tomato jar, and bake for 10 minutes at 180°C (350°F).

remove tray for the last 5 minutes or so, until pizza base is crisp.

MAKES TWO

neapolitan **pizza puffs**

These magical little footballs of dough actually puff up as you fry them. Serve with the rich tomato sauce in a bowl for dipping.

½ teaspoon dry yeast

5 tablespoons warm water

1 cup plain flour

450 grams (1 pound) ripe tomatoes

2 garlic cloves, peeled

Salt

1 tablespoon sugar

3 cups peanut oil

Fresh basil leaves, torn

dissolve yeast in 1 tablespoon of barely warm water.

combine yeast and flour in a large bowl, and slowly add remaining water.

mix until dough is firm and elastic.

knead for a few minutes, shape into a ball and let rise in a warm place for 2 hours.

pour boiling water over tomatoes, peel off skin, cut in half, squeeze to remove seeds, and chop remaining flesh.

cook tomatoes slowly with garlic, salt and sugar until soft.

scatter flour on workbench, and roll pizza dough into a log 2.5 cm (1 in) thick.

cut into 2.5 cm (1 in) pieces, and roll each piece flat into a round.

heat peanut oil and fry each pizza, turning once, until it miraculously puffs up into a pale golden orb.

drain on paper towel.

heat sauce, add basil and serve.

MAKES TWELVE

The couscous party

Couscous is to North Africa what rice is to China and pasta is to Italy: food, love, sex, mother, God and country rolled into one. It is a gloriously rich and romantic meal based on ancient Berber cooking, enriched by the crusading cultures of the Persians, the Ottomans, the Spaniards and the French.

Traditionally, the semolina grain was rolled by hand and steamed over a simmering stew, but the twentieth century calls for instant couscous, a socially acceptable fast food from your supermarket.

Couscous makes a great party buffet because it's big, easy and impressive. Bring it out on a tray piled high with glossy, jewelled zucchini, sweet carrots, nutty chickpeas and plump raisins. Surround it with pots of spicy couscous broth flavoured with tomato and saffron, and small bowls of spicy harissa (see New Basics, page 215). Add grilled meats and fish on skewers if you like.

As for dessert, peel fresh white peaches and dust with icing sugar and cinnamon, or spoon warmed honey over fresh ripe figs and toasted almonds to serve with sweet, heavy Turkish coffee or refreshing mint tea.

couscous **broth**

A delicious soup in its own right, and equally at home being spooned over couscous and vegetables.

2 tablespoons olive oil

2 onions, finely chopped

3 garlic cloves, peeled and smashed

1 teaspoon ground cumin

½ teaspoon ground coriander

1 teaspoon ground ginger

1 teaspoon sweet paprika

½ teaspoon cayenne pepper

Pinch of saffron

300 gram (11 ounce) can of tomatoes

1 teaspoon grated ginger

6 cups chicken stock or water

1 cinnamon stick

Salt

Fresh coriander for garnish

heat oil in frypan and cook onions and garlic until soft and golden.

add spices, tomatoes and fresh ginger, and cook, stirring, for 10 minutes.

add chicken stock or water, salt and cinnamon stick, and simmer gently for 20 minutes.

strain into warmed serving bowl or small individual bowls, and scatter coriander leaves on top.

SERVES TEN

couscous **with chickpeas, raisins and almonds**

A few spoonfuls of the accompanying broth with the couscous do more than just add flavour. The grains will expand to twice their size on the plate, instead of in the stomach.

1 cup dried chickpeas, soaked overnight

2 cups boiling water

450 grams (1 pound) couscous

2 tablespoons butter

Salt

6 carrots

2 tablespoons honey

6 green zucchini

6 yellow zucchini

1 cup almonds, blanched

1 cup raisins, soaked in water

1 tablespoon olive oil

couscous with chickpeas, raisins and almonds

place chickpeas in a pot of cold water, bring to boil and simmer for 30 minutes.

drain and set aside.

bring 2 cups of water to the boil, add couscous, remove from heat and allow couscous to absorb water and swell for 10 minutes.

return to heat, add butter and salt, and toss through.

turn into a lightly oiled mould, press down lightly, cover, and keep warm.

peel carrots and halve lengthwise.

bring water to boil, add salt and honey, and cook carrots and zucchini for 6 to 8 minutes until cooked but still firm.

heat a pan and dry fry almonds until golden.

add olive oil, raisins, chickpeas, and a little of the raisin soaking water, and heat through.

unmould couscous onto a warmed serving plate, arrange drained vegetables around it, and tumble raisins, almonds and chickpeas on top.

SERVES TEN

The yum cha party

There has been a Chinese revolution in the kitchens of Australia. The soy sauce now sits next to the tomato sauce, the wok is in the saucepan cupboard, and the kids are dab hands at chopsticks.

Streetwise fruit shops stock pungent fresh coriander, small brown shallots and nobbly fresh ginger, butchers sell satays, and supermarkets mini spring rolls.

The concept of yum cha, where everyone gets together over steaming baskets and platters of delicious, bite-sized morsels of food, is just made for parties. Grill a few Chinese lup cheong sausages, thinly sliced on the diagonal for an instant taste sensation.

Hunt out your nearest Asian food store and stock up on handmade siu mai dumplings and steamed buns.

Then take a tip from the noodle shop and pile dozens of chopsticks in big glasses, fill squeeze-me plastic sauce bottles with chilli sauces, and put out bulk serviette dispensers.

Appoint someone in charge of steaming, someone else in charge of frying, pour yourself a glass of wine, and wander off to enjoy your own party.

tiger prawn spring rolls

The surprise of a whole prawn wrapped in crisp golden pastry, with just its tail sticking out one end to form a handle, gives the spring roll back its spring.

6 green (raw) prawns in shell

1 tablespoon dry sherry

1 tablespoon soy sauce

1 teaspoon grated ginger

1 packet of spring roll wrappers, small

1 teaspoon cornflour mixed with 1 tablespoon cold water

Peanut oil for deep frying

Lemon wedges for serving

peel and devein prawns, leaving tail.

marinate in sherry, soy and ginger for 30 minutes.

place a prawn in one corner of a spring roll wrapper so the tail overlaps the edge.

fold the top of the wrapper down to cover prawn, then roll tightly to wrap it.

seal with a dab of the cornflour water.

heat peanut oil in wok, and fry one or two rolls at a time for 3 or 4 minutes or until golden brown.

serve with lemon wedges.

MAKES SIX

pandan **chicken**

A showy presentation of moist, spicy chicken wrapped in pandan leaves, available from all good Asian food stores.

2 lemon grass stalks, white part only, sliced

1 tablespoon grated onion

1 tablespoon grated ginger

1 garlic clove, crushed

1 fresh red chilli, sliced

1 teaspoon ground coriander

1 teaspoon five spice powder

1 teaspoon curry powder

1 teaspoon turmeric

2 teaspoons sugar

3 tablespoons coconut milk

2 chicken fillets, cut into bite-sized pieces

10 pandan leaves, fresh or frozen

Vegetable oil for deep frying

pound or blend together lemon grass, onion, ginger, garlic, chilli, coriander, five spice, curry powder, turmeric and sugar until a paste is formed.

add coconut milk and chicken, mix well and chill overnight.

cut 1 leaf into two 20 cm (8 in) strips.

place 1 tablespoon of chicken at the end of the leaf and roll up.

wrap in opposite direction with remaining leaf and secure with toothpicks.

repeat until all the chicken is wrapped.

heat oil in wok and fry each parcel for around 5 minutes.

serve piled high on a plate, and let everyone remove toothpicks and unwrap.

MAKES TEN

The cocktail party

The very words strike dread in one's heart: too much to drink, not enough to eat, and three hours of lightweight conversation. Not any more. One great cocktail, several jugs of lemon-soused mineral water, one whole cheese and plenty of bread, and neverending trays of fabulous chorizo sausage pastries will fix all that.

Buy a box of limes and make up jugfuls of Brazilian caipirissima cocktails. Then use the food processor to churn out enough choux pastry for these very effective nibbly things that you can just toss casually into the oven every half-hour or so.

Now all you have to do is make a determined effort to have a real conversation, not just small talk, and the cocktail party will be a thing of the future, and not of the past.

caipirissima

A stunning drink of fresh lime juice and white rum that is the last word on freshness. And think of all the vitamin C you're getting, if the alcohol doesn't get you first.

1 cup boiling water

1 cup sugar

10 limes, quartered

1 litre (1 quart) white rum

Crushed ice

pour water over sugar, stir until dissolved and cool.

squeeze limes into jug, then add squeezed lime quarters to jug.

add sugar syrup to the rum and ice, and stir well.

pour into individual glasses, making sure everyone gets both lime quarters and ice.

SERVES TEN

terribly **impressive chorizo puffs**

If I told you this was choux pastry, you'd turn the page. But if I told you it was quick and easy and you can bung it into the food processor, you'd love it. Well, both statements are true.

2 chorizo or spicy pork sausages

Olive oil

1 cup water

3 tablespoons butter

½ teaspoon salt

1 cup plain flour

2 free range eggs

skin sausages and crumble meat into a small frypan.

fry until meat is browned.

drain off all oil, and drain meat.

heat water, butter and salt in a heavy bottomed saucepan.

add flour all at once, as soon as water boils and butter melts.

lower heat, and stir strongly with a wooden spoon until dough leaves the sides of the pan and forms a ball.

keep cooking and stirring for a couple of minutes.

transfer dough to food processor and process for 15 seconds.

add eggs and process for 45 seconds.

stir sausage meat into mixture, and drop teaspoonfuls onto greased or non-stick tray.

bake at 200°C (400°F) for 10 to 15 minutes until golden, and serve warm.

MAKES TWENTY

199

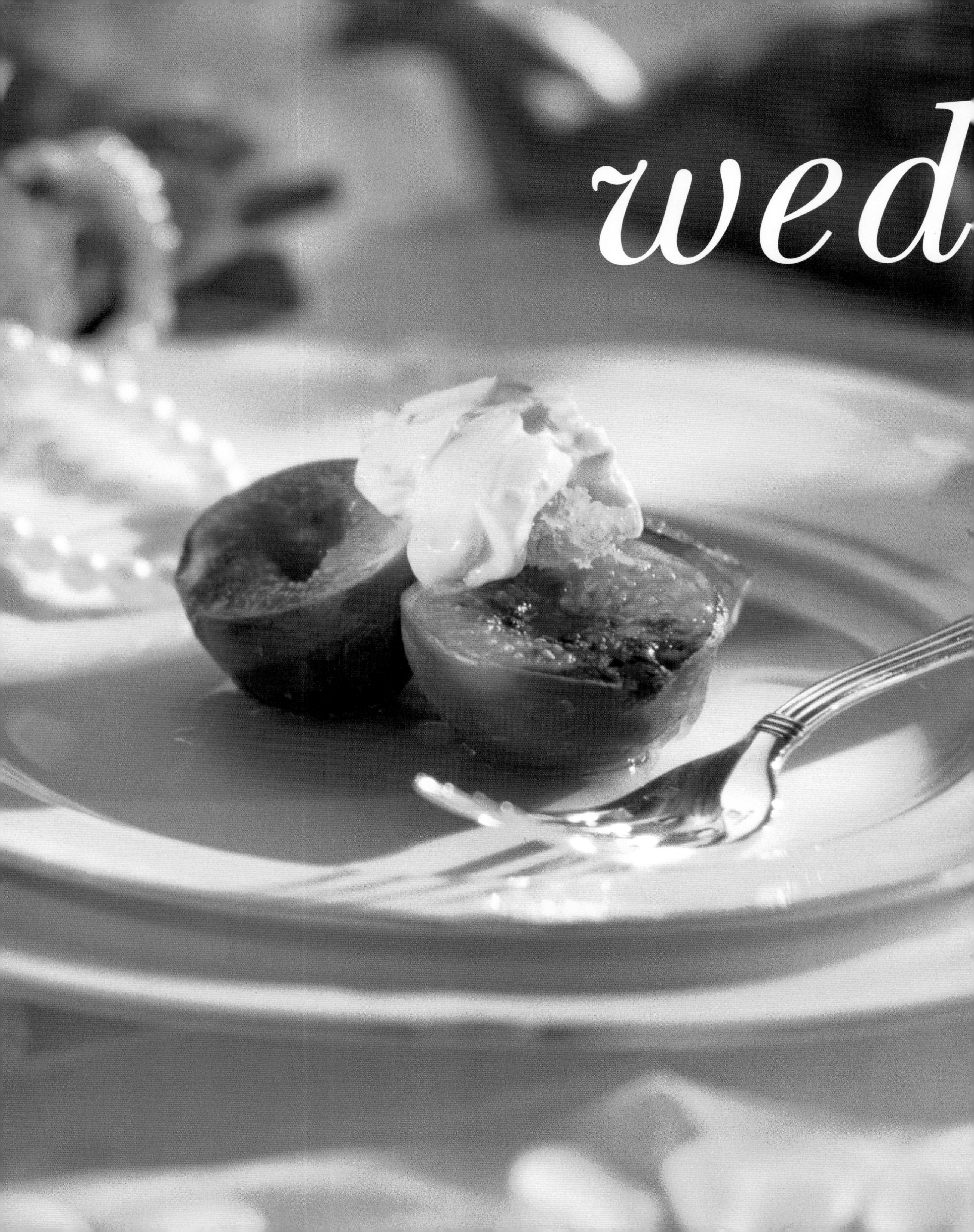
wed

Weddings are like funerals: done more for the people left behind than for the dear departed. 'We're just having something small' blushes the freshly affianced female. 'Just a few close friends.'

She's not counting on her mother, aunt, sisters and nieces, who soon find more mothers, aunts, sisters, nieces and mother-in-law to invite. Soon, her life is one long list, filled with so many whos, whats, wheres and whens, that she hardly has time to stop and wonder why.

If it isn't who to invite, it's what to wear. Then it's The Date. The Ring. The Bouquet. The Best Man. The Flowers. The Photographer. The Honeymoon. Her new mother-in-law wants the whole thing videotaped. Sooner or later, talk turns to The Reception, and, finally, The Menu.

If as much effort went into choosing our marriage partners as goes into our weddings, the divorce rate of western society would be halved.

Enter The New Wedding. There is only one golden rule, and that is to be true to yourself. If you dislike pomp and ceremony, dispense with it. If you don't normally attend church, avoid hypocrisy and get married in a beautiful garden, on an island, or in a rainforest.

There are no laws that say you have to wear a white dress, eat mousse, read dirty telegrams, or drink cheap wine. The very best wedding receptions are those designed as great parties first, and receptions second. Think past the hackneyed venues, and take over your favourite restaurant, or get married where you first fell in love.

Whatever your theme, the food should be all things bright and beautiful, on this day of days (you'll get used to clichés like that). Forget the salmon mousse/beef wellington/chocolate mousse menu of your mother's day, and go for golden saffron pasta flecked with fresh salmon caviar, an updated Russian coulibiac of a whole salmon in a golden crust of brioche pastry, and warm grilled figs drenched in honey. Create bridal bouquets of edible green leaves, spray them with a champagne vinaigrette, and serve them as salads.

Or lay out tables of all your favourite foods, as long as they are free of fuss, like fresh oysters, prawns, hams on the bone, and big platters of baby pizze and chargrilled vegetables. Or create an all-white wedding breakfast, from a creamy brandade of salt cod to champagne risotto and white chocolate cake. Or just beg your favourite restaurant to do your favourite dish, two hundred times over. As for the table — if you have one — add a little fantasy with gold hearts, lashings of tulle, sweet sauternes, and honey-scented candles, and you'll have a wedding breakfast to remember.

It's just a shame you have to get married in order to enjoy it.

grilled figs with
cinnamon
mascarpone
RECIPE 125

201

Christ

MAS

Christmas day is a day of sharing, caring, giving, getting, talking, cooking, eating, drinking, dressing up and cleaning up. It's a day of wonder, of hope, and of anticipation. It can also be the day the balloon bursts in your face, the day you didn't get a single present you wouldn't immediately bury in the garden, and, if you are on your own, the longest day of the year.

Christmas is a day that children look forward to and adults dread. A day of martyrdom in the kitchen and magnanimity in the face of utter chaos. Let's face it, it is the one day of the year when you cannot avoid your relatives.

So you may as well relax, enjoy yourself, and have a great meal, in spite of it all. If all you want is an easy, breezy meal of fast, fresh and festive food, then round up Santa's little helpers and get it all done for you.

Order a whole smoked fish for the centre of the table, and serve plenty of hot toast and horseradish-spiked sour cream.

Lay out cold hams, big, bold, bright platters of antipasto, salads, fresh oysters and prawns, and as many dips and sauces as there are presents under the tree.

Make strawberry wine by blending a punnet of strawberries, pushing them through a sieve, and topping the juices with chilled dry white wine and a dash of strawberry liqueur.

Finish with a fragrant Italian pannetone cake and coffee (and leave enough cake to grill a few slices for Boxing Day breakfast), and ruby-red berries heaped high in glass bowls, layered with yoghurt and scattered with icing sugar.

Gift-wrap your Christmas table in metres of white tulle, tied in big bows at each corner, or keep it sweet and simple with long strands of fresh green ivy and bright red baubles borrowed from the tree.

Then all you have to do is fill the bathtub with ice and bottles of champagne and mineral water, and have a very merry Christmas.

n e w **B A S I C S**

Once upon a time, you had to know how to make a

bechamel sauce. Now, it's more important to preserve your own lemons. Then, you had to master a velouté sauce, and know the difference between béarnaise and hollandaise. Now, it's twenty ways with **sun-dried tomatoes**. Then, it was mornay. Now, it's cumin mayonnaise. The only constants that remain are good chicken stock (close to God), and good fish and vegetable stocks. Even pastry is lighter, easier and faster.

In the meantime, new technology changes the way in which we do things. Cooking utensils change. While a heavy bottomed cast iron pot is still just as handy today as it was one hundred years ago, the new essential is a good, solid **non-stick pan**.

Good knives are **more important** than ever before. Food 'processors' and blenders have their uses, but we need to keep sharpening our cutting and carving skills as well, or our food will be **processed to death**.

My most useful kitchen companions are **paper towels** (to wipe, to drain, to skim off fat), tea towels (as many as possible), sieves and strainers, whisks, big stainless steel bowls (wonderful for whisking a vinaigrette before tossing in the leaves), my **well-seasoned wok**, a Chinese cleaver (cleaves straight through a chicken, and hard-to-cut pumpkin), and good, clean, fast, honest heat.

Heat a wok or frying pan first, before adding any oil, and you'll use half the amount. Industrial-strength heat is the secret of many of your favourite meals out, so don't be scared by it at home.

Malay cooks speak of the **wok-taste** of keuh teow noodles that comes from a fierce, clean heat, while the Cantonese talk of dishes having **'wok hei'** or the 'breath of the wok', from a masterly juggling of time and heat.

The final essential in every kitchen is, of course, **time**. Time to get organised, time to enjoy what you are doing, and time to allow the food to develop its **full flavour**. And with a few of these **new basics** in your repertoire, you should be able to spend more time at the table, having a good time.

roasted **red pepper sauce**

A brilliant sauce, in both colour and flavour. Serve it with grilled prawns or a barbecued fish, draped over vegetables, swirled through a vegetable soup or drizzled over roasted lamb.

4 red capsicums

1 tablespoon olive oil

300 gram (11 ounce) can tomatoes, drained

Pinch of salt

Pinch of cayenne pepper

drizzle olive oil over capsicums in baking tray and roast in 200°C (400°F) oven for 30 minutes, until skin bubbles and darkens.

place in covered bowl for 10 minutes.

peel off skin under cold running water.

cut open, keeping any juices, and discarding skin and seeds.

place flesh, juice, and tomatoes in food processor and blend.

pour mixture through a sieve, pushing against the mesh to extract maximum colour and flavour.

add salt and cayenne pepper to taste.

SERVES FOUR TO SIX

preserved **lemons**

Magical, mysterious Moroccan food depends on the unique flavour of these lemons, preserved in salt and lemon juice. Do them now, and they will be soft, mellow, and almost voluptuous in a month's time.

20 lemons

1 cup of coarse sea salt

2 sticks of cinnamon

10 cloves

12 black peppercorns

3 bay leaves

Extra lemon juice if required

clean lemons and cut in quarters lengthwise, leaving the end uncut.

sprinkle salt on the inside flesh, close up fruit, and place in a large sterilised jar.

repeat until all lemons and salt are used.

push lemons down hard into the jar to release the juice, slipping the spices and leaves in as you go.

top jar with extra lemon juice to cover.

leave in a warm place for 30 days, turning upside down for a few seconds each day.

keep jar topped with lemon juice. Preserved in this way, they will last for months.

rinse lemons before use, discarding flesh and using the skin.

MAKES ONE VERY LARGE JAR

olive **tapenade**

Yes, you can always buy a good tapenade, but people are terribly impressed when you announce you make your own. I can't think why, because it's dead easy.

2 cups of black olives, stoned

4 anchovy fillets

1 dried chilli, crushed

2 tablespoons small capers, rinsed

A good squeeze of lemon

Freshly ground black pepper

3 tablespoons olive oil

blend olives, anchovies, chilli, capers, lemon juice and pepper in food processor.

add olive oil gradually, to make a rich, dark paste.

store in an airtight jar in refrigerator for up to a month.

to make it your very own, you can add a few sun-dried tomatoes, or a can of tuna in oil, some Dijon mustard, a dash of cognac, or fresh parsley or basil. Or you can keep it chunky rather than blended to a paste.

serve with pasta, focaccia, and hard-boiled eggs, or on grilled fish, chicken or lamb.

S E R V E S   F O U R   T O   S I X

extra **deluxe olive tapenade**

A magnificent, irresistible flavour that inspires cold roast chicken, lemon risotto, roasted vegetables or plain old grilled bread. From Robert Carrier's Feasts of Provence.

2 tablespoons olive oil

3 rashers lean bacon, finely chopped

1 purple-skinned onion, finely chopped

2 garlic cloves

2 cups black olives, stoned and chopped

½ red capsicum, cut into tiny dice

4 anchovy fillets, chopped

2 tablespoons chopped flat-leaf parsley

1 tablespoon chopped fresh thyme

2 tablespoons small capers, rinsed

1 dried red chilli, crushed

Freshly ground pepper

heat olive oil and fry bacon.

add onion and garlic and cook for 10 minutes, stirring.

add olives, capsicum, anchovies, parsley, thyme and capers and cook, stirring, for 5 minutes.

add crushed chilli and pepper, and leave for flavours to infuse.

S E R V E S   F O U R

chermoula **marinade for fish and seafood**

A spiky, tangy marinade that makes the most of whole fish, prawns, bugs, scallops and squid. Use the remaining marinade as a sauce.

Handful of fresh coriander

Handful of fresh parsley

2 garlic cloves, smashed

1 teaspoon ground cumin

1 teaspoon ground coriander

1 teaspoon ground paprika

Juice of 2 lemons

Grated rind of 1 lemon

2 tablespoons olive oil

toss all ingredients into food processor and blend, or chop and mix by hand. .

M A K E S   O N E   C U P

pesto

Although pesto is becoming a generic term for all manner of fresh herb and nut pastes the original must be considered the best. If I don't have at least two jars of basil pesto in the house, I get twitchy.

2 tablespoons pine nuts

2 cups fresh basil leaves

2 garlic cloves, crushed

3 tablespoons pecorino or parmigiano, grated

½ cup olive oil

Salt

toast pine nuts briefly in a hot dry pan until they turn a touch golden.

combine basil, pine nuts, garlic, cheese and salt in food processor and blend to a smooth paste.

add oil slowly with the motor running.

store in an airtight jar in refrigerator, where it will last for a month or so.

serve a spoonful in your favourite vegetable soup, into a potato salad, or onto pasta or gnocchi.

continue topping jar with olive oil as you use it, or the exposed bits will go brown.

MAKES ONE GOOD-SIZED JAR

tunisian **capsicum relish**

A gorgeous red relish that is hot to trot with chilli, garlic and lemon juice. Serve with polenta, baked ricotta or grilled focaccia.

3 red capsicums

1 red chilli

2 garlic cloves

1 teaspoon ground coriander

Juice of 1 lemon

1 tablespoon olive oil

halve capsicums and chilli, and deseed.

combine with garlic in processor and blend.

stir in coriander, lemon juice and olive oil.

MAKES ONE CUP

lemon **curd**

This thick, tangy, golden, buttery curd is delicious on grilled bread, in tiny tarts, or spread over lemon cake.

140 grams (5 ounces) butter

1 cup sugar

3 free range eggs

Juice of 3 lemons

Grated rind of 1 lemon

melt butter in a double-boiler, or in a heatproof bowl sitting in simmering water.

add sugar and stir with a wooden spoon to dissolve.

beat the eggs and strain them through a sieve into the mixture, stirring.

add lemon juice and continue to stir over low heat for 15 minutes or so, until the mixture thickens.

pour into a clean glass jar, cool, and chill.

MAKES ONE GOOD-SIZED JAR

moroccan **lemon yoghurt sauce**

A tangy, refreshing side dish for meatballs, grilled vegetables, and roasted poussin.

2 preserved lemons (see New Basics, page 208)
1 cup natural yoghurt

drain and rinse 2 preserved lemons, remove and discard flesh, and chop skin into tiny dice.
mix with yoghurt and serve.

MAKES ONE CUP

slow-roasted **tomatoes**

The slow roasting intensifies the flavour of tomatoes, making them delicious accessories to grilled meats, smashed onto grilled bread, or plumped into the middle of a bowl of soup.

10 basil leaves
2 tablespoons olive oil
6 tomatoes
Salt and freshly ground pepper

tear leaves and infuse in oil for 1 hour.
place clean tomatoes on baking tray, drizzle with olive oil, and sprinkle with salt and pepper.
bake at 160°C (320°F) for 1 hour, until they soften.

SERVES SIX

polenta

Polenta is one of the oldest, simplest and downright nicest dishes in Italy. You can serve it very simply steaming hot, as you would mashed potato, or leave it to set in a pan for later use.

2 cups water
½ cup polenta
½ teaspoon salt
1 tablespoon butter
1 tablespoon grated parmigiano

bring water to boil in your heaviest bottomed pot.
when bubbling, add polenta and salt in a steady stream, beating and stirring constantly with a wooden spoon to avoid any lumps forming.
reduce heat, and simmer, stirring, scraping polenta down from the sides.
after 20 or 30 minutes, when you can see that the individual grains have dissolved, stir in butter and cheese, and heat through for 3 minutes.
pour onto a warmed serving platter and serve immediately, or pour into a lightly oiled tray, cool and refrigerate.
you can then slice polenta and grill it over high heat until golden, to serve with chargrilled meats and vegetables.

SERVES FOUR

breadcrumbs

Breadcrumbs are as good as the bread you use, so use your favourite sourdough, crustiest French baguette, or tastiest light rye.

tear day-old bread into chunks and whizz it in the food processor until it is a happy mix of fine and coarse.

spread crumbs out on baking trays and bake on the bottom shelf of the oven at 150°C (300°F) for 15 minutes until dry.

store in airtight jars.

pizza **base**

An easy, biscuity pizza base that will turn your kitchen into a pizzeria. For a nice, crisp base, heat a clean terracotta tile in the oven for 10 minutes, and place the pizza on it to bake.

50 grams (2 ounces) butter

350 grams (12 ounces) self-raising flour

Up to 1 cup milk

1 teaspoon lemon juice

preheat oven to 200°C (400°F).

cube butter and process in blender with flour on a stop-start, stop-start basis until it resembles fine breadcrumbs.

add milk and lemon juice, and stop-start until it gathers into a ball. (Throw in more flour if too wet).

turn dough onto floured board and knead lightly, and roll or pat out to round or square shape.

pinch edge slightly to raise it.

add your choice of toppings, drizzle with a little olive oil, and bake for 15 minutes.

remove tray and bake for another 5 minutes or so, until base is crisp and topping is perfect.

MAKES ONE PIZZA BASE

vegetable **stock**

A light, fresh base for sauces or soups which is an absolute dream to have ready and waiting in your refrigerator or freezer.

2 tomatoes

1 tablespoon butter

2 brown onions, finely chopped

2 carrots, finely chopped

2 celery stalks, finely chopped

6 parsley stalks

cut tomatoes in half, squeeze out the seeds.

melt butter in heavy bottomed pot, add vegetables, parsley stalks and tomatoes, and cook for 5 minutes.

add 6 cups of boiling water, bring back to the boil, and simmer for 10 minutes.

strain stock through a sieve, cool and refrigerate.

MAKES ONE AND A HALF LITRES

(ONE AND A HALF QUARTS)

fish **stock**

Having fish stock in the freezer is real social security. Making it is remarkably quick and easy, so now there's no excuse.

1 onion

1 carrot

1 celery stalk

1 garlic clove

1 leek, white part only

1 tablespoon olive oil

1 kilo (2 pounds) fish heads and bones

1 cup dry white wine

10 peppercorns

2 bay leaves

1 litre water

chop onion, carrot, celery, garlic and leek.

heat oil in large pot and cook vegetables over low heat for about 10 minutes until they 'sweat'.

add rinsed fish heads and bones, wine, peppercorns and bay leaves and bring to the boil.

add water and return to the boil.

simmer over low heat for 10 to 15 minutes, no longer.

strain through a strainer lined with muslin, pushing down on bones to release the utmost juices.

MAKES ONE LITRE (ONE QUART)

chicken **stock**

A gleaming, fat-free chicken stock is the pride of any kitchen and the basis of hundreds of ideas. It's cheap to make, with your time being the only real expense.

2 kilo (4 pounds) chicken bones

3 litres (3 quarts) water

2 onions

2 carrots

1 celery stalk

3 parsley stalks

8 peppercorns

1 bay leaf

1 leek, white part only

rinse chicken bones and place them in your largest pot with water.

bring to the boil and skim off any froth that rises to the surface.

add remaining ingredients and simmer for 3 hours, uncovered, skimming occasionally.

strain into a bowl, discarding bones and vegetables, and chill overnight to allow any fat to rise to the surface.

when ready to use or freeze, remove fat.

if you want a more intense flavour, cook again at a high simmer to reduce the liquid by half.

MAKES THREE LITRES

(THREE QUARTS)

sweet **onion marmalade**

This is a beautiful condiment to serve with chargrilled liver or lamb, or just dobbed into a creamy white bean or vegetable soup.

6 onions

2 chillies

2 tablespoons olive oil

2 tablespoons brown sugar

½ cup water

1 tablespoon red wine vinegar

1 cup dry white wine

2 bay leaves

2 cloves

Salt and freshly ground pepper

peel and chop onions, halve and deseed chillies.

heat oil and gently cook onion and chilli until soft.

add sugar and water and cook for 20 minutes until golden.

add vinegar, wine, bay leaves and cloves and cook over low heat, stirring occasionally, for a further 15 minutes or so until mixture looks jammy.

cool, and store in an airtight jar in refrigerator for up to a week.

MAKES ONE JAR

fresh **mint chutney**

This is like a breath of fresh air in the middle of an Indian curry dinner. But there is no reason why you can't serve it at an un-Indian barbecue, or with cold boiled meats.

1 cup mint leaves

4 spring onions with greens

1 garlic clove

2 fresh green chillies

3 tablespoons vinegar

Salt

½ teaspoon sugar

throw everything into the food processor and blend.

taste for salt or sugar.

tip into a small bowl and serve.

MAKES ONE CUP

nuoc **cham sauce**

This sauce is to Vietnam what soy sauce is to China and fish sauce is to Thailand. Vary the ingredients to your taste, and go for a dip.

2 tablespoons sugar

2 tablespoons warm water

1 garlic clove, crushed

2 tablespoons fish sauce (nuoc mam or nam pla)

2 tablespoons lime or lemon juice

1 slice lime or lemon, segmented

2 red chillies, sliced

1 tablespoon white vinegar

stir sugar into water until dissolved.

combine with all ingredients.

leave all the chunky bits in. They look great.

serve as a dipping sauce for fresh spring rolls, grilled chicken, lamb and pork, meatballs, and so on.

MAKES ONE CUP

harissa

This stuff is hot! Add a little of it to your couscous broth, to red pepper soups, to vegetable stews and to homemade mayonnaise, and you'll soon be addicted.

4 dried red chillies

1 teaspoon caraway seed

½ teaspoon cumin seeds

½ teaspoon coriander seeds

1 teaspoon dried mint

2 garlic cloves, crushed

½ teaspoon salt

1 tablespoon water

3 tablespoons olive oil

soak chillies in hot water for 1 hour.

grind spices together in a coffee grinder reserved for your spices, not your coffee.

drain chillies, pat dry and chop.

blend chillies with garlic, spices, and salt until a thick paste forms.

add water and olive oil, mix well and store in refrigerator in a well-sealed jar.

MAKES ONE JAR

mayonnaise

Add half a teaspoon of cumin powder for cumin mayo, a teaspoon of garlic purée for garlic mayo, a teaspoon of harissa sauce for chilli mayo, etcetera. You get the general idea.

2 egg yolks

Juice of 1 lemon

1½ cups light olive oil

Salt and freshly ground pepper

blend egg yolks and lemon juice in food processor.

keep motor running while you ever so slowly pour in the olive oil, drop by drop.

after the first half cup has been absorbed, you can drizzle it in slightly faster, teaspoon by teaspoon, until all oil is absorbed.

taste for salt and pepper, and add more lemon juice if you like.

MAKES ONE JAR

rosemary oil

Australian chef Greg Brown uses rosemary oil to drizzle over white beans and tender baby lamb. Use this same method to infuse any olive oil with any herb, and you will have its intense flavour at your disposal all year round for salads, vegetables and meats.

10 branches of fresh rosemary

1 cup extra virgin olive oil

strip branches of leaves.

bash leaves with a meat mallet.

warm oil, add leaves, and leave to simmer, not boil, for 30 minutes.

do not leave the kitchen to answer the phone, the door, or any member of the family, no matter how dear.

let cool, and leave overnight.

strain into a sterilised bottle, and cork.

MAKES ONE CUP

corn tortillas

Mexican corn tortillas are made from dried corn flour called masa harina, available from Mexican food specialists. Roll them around grilled meat and salad as if for souvlaki, or serve them under beans and eggs.

2 cups masa harina flour

1 cup warm water

mix flour and water with your hands until dough is firm and moist.

if it is still dry, add extra water, 1 tablespoon at a time.

let dough rest for 15 minutes.

divide dough into 12 portions and shape into small balls.

place each ball between two sheets of greaseproof paper or 2 plastic sandwich bags, and use a rolling pin to flatten into a 15 cm (6 in) circle.

peel 1 sheet or bag from tortilla, and place uncovered side down on a medium-hot ungreased frypan.

as it heats and softens, peel off the other sheet or bag.

cook for 1 minute, turn and cook for 2 or 3 minutes, until it is dry, soft, and light brown.

trim if desired, and keep warm and well covered while you cook remaining tortillas.

MAKES TWELVE

olive and rosemary bread

This biscuity, rosemary-scented bread is delicious with soups, antipasto or as a burger.

375 grams (13 ounces) plain flour

1 teaspoon salt

1 teaspoon baking powder

1 onion, thinly sliced

1 cup olives, stoned

2 tablespoons fresh rosemary, chopped

1 tablespoon grated parmigiano

2 tablespoons melted butter

Up to ½ cup milk

Extra melted butter

sift flour, salt and baking powder into a large bowl.

add onion slices, pitted olives, rosemary and cheese, and mix through with your hands.

melt butter until frothy, and add to flour with milk, mixing to form a smooth dough. If too dry, add a little water.

knead dough a few times in the bowl, form into a ball, cover, and rest overnight in the fridge.

divide dough into 6 or 8 balls, and roll each ball out on a lightly floured bench to a rough circle.

brush with melted butter and place on a greased or non-stick baking sheet in 200°C (400°F) oven for 10 minutes, then turn over and bake for 5 minutes.

leave to cool or eat hot.

MAKES SIX TO EIGHT ROUNDS

fresh *yoghurt* **cheese**

Delicious when spread on crusty bread, dolloped into pasta or an omelette, or formed into small balls and kept in virgin olive oil. You can flavour the yoghurt with herbs or spices before or after draining, or leave pure and simple.

2 cups natural yoghurt
Virgin olive oil
Sprigs of rosemary

stir yoghurt until smooth, then tip onto a square of clean, dampened muslin, and hang over a deep bowl.

leave to hang overnight.

unwrap cheese and use in whatever shape or form you wish.

to preserve it, shape cheese into walnut-sized balls in the palms of your hands, and drop each cheese ball gently into a glass jar half-filled with olive oil.

tuck sprigs of rosemary down the side of the jar, and top with remaining olive oil.

cover and leave in a cool place for at least 2 days.

MAKES TWELVE BALLS

crisped **vine leaves**

These are a small Mediterranean frivolity to use as a conversation-stopping accessory to a Moroccan or Middle Eastern dish. Lebanese-born Mod Med chef Greg Malouf serves them with fetta, with grilled fish, or with cheese.

10 vine leaves, packed in oil or salt
1 tablespoon olive oil

rinse vine leaves, and gently pat dry with paper towel.

brush leaves on both sides with a very light slick of olive oil.

bake at 200°C (400°F) for 1 minute, watching closely.

turn leaves and bake for another minute, taking care to avoid burning.

set aside on cake rack to cool.

MAKES TEN

grilled **tomato sauce**

A lovely way to keep the sun-drenched flavour of ripe, fresh tomatoes with you a little longer. Serve with fresh basil leaves.

4 large ripe tomatoes
2 leeks
2 garlic cloves
2 tablespoons olive oil
1 teaspoon red wine vinegar
½ teaspoon cayenne pepper
Salt and freshly ground pepper

grill the tomatoes whole, until the skin blackens and the tomato softens.

cool, peel away skin and chop flesh.

heat olive oil, add leeks and garlic and cook for 5 minutes until leek is soft.

add tomatoes and cook for 5 minutes.

add vinegar, cayenne, salt and pepper, and leave to cool.

MAKES ONE CUP

sweet *garlic* crostini

A revelation to anyone scared of garlic's harsh sting and lingering smell. Make it whenever you can find or grow small, young heads (quorms) of garlic, and serve their sweet, soft purée with roasted meats, grilled fish, potatoes, on the side of soups or tucked into salads.

4 small heads (quorms) of garlic

1 tablespoon olive oil

Salt and freshly ground pepper

Sprigs of fresh thyme

Sprigs of fresh rosemary

1 long bread stick

cut each garlic head in half right across the cloves.

rub garlic with a little olive oil.

season cut halves with salt and pepper and sandwich garlic back together with herbs pressed in the middle.

wrap each garlic loosely in foil and bake at 180°C (350°F) for 1 to 2 hours, until the garlic feels very soft to the touch.

cut bread stick into thin slices, and lay on baking tray. Brush with a little oil and bake until crisp, around 10 minutes.

unwrap garlic, squeeze cloves onto crostini, and serve.

MAKES TWELVE

lemonade

Forget your politically correct mineral water for one moment, and make a good, old-fashioned lemonade.

1 cup sugar

Rind of 2 lemons

5 cups cold water

¾ cup fresh lemon juice

combine sugar, lemon rind and 1 cup of water and simmer for 7 or 8 minutes.

cool, and strain into jug.

add juice, remaining water, and chill.

MAKES ONE LITRE

(ONE QUART)

mint tea

Fragrant and refreshing, mint tea is heaven on earth after lunch on a lazy, sunny afternoon, served with little sweetmeats or almond biscuits.

3 teaspoons green tea

Fresh mint leaves

Sugar cubes to taste

place green tea in a pot, and top with boiling water.

strain and top with extra boiling water.

add leaves and sugar cubes, and leave for 2 or 3 minutes.

slip a sprig of fresh mint into each small glass, and serve.

SERVES FOUR

vanilla **custard**

A divinely rich but surprisingly light crème anglaise, dotted with the fine seed of the noble vanilla bean. Add a tablespoon of cognac, brandy, dark rum or your favourite liqueur as it cools, for a little extra spirit.

10 egg yolks
140 grams (5 ounces) castor sugar
1 litre (1 quart) milk
1 vanilla bean, split lengthwise

whisk egg yolks and sugar together until pale and creamy.

bring milk and vanilla bean to boil, then scrape seeds from bean into milk and discard bean.

pour milk in a slow, steady stream into the egg mixture, whisking slowly.

when combined, return to pan and cook very, very gently, stirring all the while with a wooden spoon for around 15 minutes, until custard thickens enough to drip slowly from the spoon.

if mixture starts to set, remove from heat, strain, cool, and return to a gentler heat.

strain into a bowl resting in a sink or basin of ice cold water.

cool and chill.

MAKES ONE LITRE

(ONE QUART)

shortcrust **pastry**

A quick and easy food processor pastry that's perfect for sweet tarts.

¾ cup plain flour, sifted
115 grams (4 ounces) butter, chilled and cut into pieces
2 teaspoons sugar
3 tablespoons ice cold water

place flour, butter and sugar in food processor.

process until the mixture resembles coarse crumbs, about 10 seconds.

add ice cold water and process on a stop-start basis until the pastry just begins to hold together (about 6 to 8 times), before it turns into a ball.

wrap in waxed paper and chill for 1 hour before proceeding.

if too sticky, sprinkle with extra flour and knead gently.

MAKES PASTRY FOR ONE TART

index

new food bibliography

Bocuse, Paul. **French Home Cooking**, Grafton Books, London 1989.

Campbell, Dolly. **I Hate To Cook**, Mandarin, Melbourne, 1991.

Carrier, Robert. **Taste of Morocco**, Century Hutchinson Limited, Melbourne 1987.

—— **Feasts of Provence**, Allen & Unwin, London 1993.

David, Elizabeth. **French Provincial Cooking**, Penguin, Middlesex 1970.

Devi, Yamuna. **The Art of Indian Vegetarian Cooking**, Century Hutchinson Limited, London 1987.

Dupleix, Jill and Miller, Jane. **The Women's Cookbook**, William Heinemann Australia, Melbourne 1992.

Harris, Valentina. **Recipes From An Italian Farmhouse**, Conran Octopus, London 1989.

Jaffrey, Madhur. **A Taste of India**, Pavilion/Michael Joseph, 1985.

Roden, Claudia. **A New Book of Middle Eastern Food**, Penguin Cookery Library, Middlesex 1985.

Routhier, Nicole. **The Foods of Vietnam**, Stewart, Tabori & Chang, New York 1989.

Scotto, Elisabeth. **The Encyclopaedia of French Cooking**, Octopus Books Limited, London 1982.

Shulman, Martha Rose. **Mediterranean Light**, Bantam Books, New York 1989.

Solomon, Charmaine. **Charmaine Solomon's Thai Cookbook**, Greenhouse Publications, Melbourne 1989.

Wells, Patricia. **Bistro Cooking**, Workman Publishing, New York 1989.

White, Marco Pierre. **White Heat**, Pyramid Books, London 1990.

thank you

To Liz Nicholson for her delicious new design and typography. More thanks go to Fran Hernon and everyone at *New Woman*, Sue Hines and Louise Stirling of Reed Books, Le Madri (New York), Le Cygne (Rome), Maria Battaglia (Verona), Marco Pierre White (London) and the International Olive Oil Council for inspiration and information. And most of all to Terry Durack, for his neverending ideas, taste, support and love.

photo credits

The reason *New Food* looks as good as it tastes is due to the enormous talents of John Hay, Mark Chew, Jacqui Henshaw, Simon Griffiths, Glenn Gibson, Jack Sarafian and Arunas. I am eternally grateful to them for being so good to work with, and for the use of their work in *New Food*.

Cover photo by Mark Chew

John Hay, *pages 4, 5, 10, 12, 16, 21, 24, 29, 32, 37, 51, 63, 64, 65, 68, 85, 88, 93, 98, 99, 102, 104, 107, 110, 122, 128, 132, 137, 140, 141, 145, 146, 148, 151, 152, 157, 161, 164, 168, 172, 177, 178, 180, 183, 186, 189, 191, 193, 205, 220*

Mark Chew, *pages 27, 28, 33, 40, 42, 44, 49, 53, 54, 58, 61, 69, 74, 77, 80, 101, 119, 121, 124, 125, 134, 174, 184, 196, 200, 204*

Jacqui Henshaw, *pages 20, 72, 91, 115, 153*

Simon Griffiths, *pages 56, 192, 204, 206*

Glenn Gibson, *pages 116, 127*

Jack Sarafian, *page 96*

Arunas, *author photo, pages 1, 2*